Exposing
Satan's
Devices

by
Betty Miller

First Edition Published 1980
Second Printing 1982
Third Printing 1983
Fourth Printing 1984
Fifth Printing 1987
Sixth Printing 1988
Seventh Printing 1989
Eighth Printing 1991
Ninth Printing 1994
Tenth Printing 2003
Print On Demand

Exposing Satan's Devices

ISBN 1-57149-021-3

CHRIST UNLIMITED MINISTRIES, INC.
Pastor R.S. "Bud" Miller - Publisher
P.O. Box 850
Dewey, Arizona 86327

Printed in U.S.A.

Scripture quotations are taken from the King James Version
unless otherwise indicated.

Contents

Section 3: The World of Demons

Preface

Greetings in the name of our Lord Jesus Christ:

I present this book to the body of Christ as the Holy Spirit presented it to me. I challenge you to allow God's Spirit of truth, and the Bible, to test the accuracy of the words within these pages. This book, part of the Overcoming Life Series, is also addressed to all seekers of truth who know not THE CHRIST UNLIMITED, as it would be my privilege to introduce you to Him.

During the early years of the ministry, I struggled to learn how to hear the voice of God. Once, while nervously waiting to speak before a large audience, and not being sure on what subject I should speak, I posed to the Lord in prayer this question: "Lord, what am I going to say to all these people?" In my spirit, I heard Him very clearly reply, "Betty, I was hoping you would not say anything, as I really wanted to speak." Yes, He wants to speak through us, as we yield to His Spirit. Submitting to the Lord and the guidance of the Holy Spirit, I found, was not only possible, but the only way He wants us to minister. **For it is not ye that speak, but the Spirit of your Father which speaketh in you (Matthew 10:20).**

This book is a gift from the Holy Spirit. I take no credit for it. If something within these pages blesses you, enlightens you, brings you closer to the Lord, releases you from fear or bondage, or heals or delivers you, then please lift your voice in praise to the precious Savior of our souls, Jesus Christ our Lord! On the other hand, if you find some of these things difficult to receive, hard to understand, or totally heretical from your viewpoint, would you also look to the Lord and ask Him if it could possibly be the truth? With an open and honest heart, will you ask God to change any pre-conceived ideas, and be free from traditions to receive of Him, His truth? His truth always brings freedom, never bondage. **And ye shall know the truth, and the truth shall make you free (John 8:32).**

In walking with the Lord, I have found we must obey the things we feel He is speaking to us. In my personal life, I used to be fearful of speaking for the Lord because I was so afraid of missing Him and making mistakes. (He, of course, has now delivered me of all my fears. Praise Him!) He encouraged me not to quit because of mistakes when He spoke these words to me: "Betty, if I receive the glory and praise for all the things that are a blessing to people, I also receive the responsibility for your mistakes, as long as you are striving to please me. I am able to make even those work for your good." **And we know that all things work together for good to them that love God, to them who are the called according to his purpose (Romans 8:28).** We serve a wonderful, loving God, who encourages us to follow and obey Him that we might be blessed, and in turn bless others!

This book was written as an act of obedience to the Lord, whom I dearly love. I consider it an honor to write for Him. Years ago, when I was in prayer, the Lord spoke that I was to write a book, but I never felt it was God's timing, nor did I feel the unction or anointing to begin this work until now. Over the past year God has performed a series of miracles to confirm that it is now His time, and has made the arrangements for this to become a reality.

I pray that this book, along with the Overcoming Life Series, may help you learn to walk closer to our Lord, as He is THE CHRIST UNLIMITED!

I am, by His love,
A handmaiden of the Lord,

Betty Miller
February, 1980

If any man will do his will, he shall know of the doctrine, whether it be of God, or whether I speak of myself (John 7:17).

Foreword

It just seemed natural that I would do the foreword on this book since my wife, Betty, and myself, are "one flesh." God, through the Holy Spirit, has given by revelation to Betty many truths of His Word, which have been set forth in this book.

The Lord spoke to Betty about ten years ago that she was to write a book for Him, and that He would arrange the right time and place to write it. Betty simply took this vision and set it aside until God began to "quicken" her spirit to bring it forth. One morning, very early, Betty awakened, and began to write as the Lord dictated to her. In giving her this small initial portion of the book, he showed her how, by submitting to His Spirit, and completely yielding to Him, He would feed to her the message He wanted to share with the body of Christ. He also revealed how quickly and easily it would be completed. The messages that God has given in this Overcoming Life Series are to all who desire to become "overcomers" and be "conformed to the image of His son" (**Romans 8:29**). Our Lord is not satisfied that a person remains a "babe" in Christ, but longs for each "babe" to grow to maturity. He desires that we should strive to become overcomers, live the overcoming life, and claim the promises of the inheritance of all things that are to be given to the overcomers.

I thank God that He has allowed me to share such close love and companionship with Betty. I know that within her heart she has no personal ambitions, no personal ends to achieve. Betty has simply been doing the will of the Father in the writing of this anointed book. May the Lord bless you with this book, as He has blessed us in being a part of His work.

Yours in Christ,

Pastor R.S. (Bud) Miller

He that overcometh shall inherit all things; and I will be his God and he shall be my son (Revelation 21:7).

Credits & Acknowledgments

ALL PRAISE AND CREDIT
GOES TO **THE CHRIST UNLIMITED**!

Truly Christ, the Father, and the Holy Spirit, are to be praised, not only for this book, but for our very lives. His sacrifice on Calvary made it possible to know Him and all the members of God's family.

As with the printing of any book, there are lots of people responsible for the words on these pages, physical words as well as spiritual words. All the people that have ever been a part of my life, all the people that have prayed and supported this ministry, my friends and my family have truly contributed to this work. Special credit should be given to my husband, Bud, whose faithful and loving prayers, encouragement, leadership, and love are a big part of this book. Also, to everyone whose books and articles I've read, to the ministers of the Gospel, whose sermons I've heard, I express my gratitude. For each has contributed, in some measure, to this book. The list is endless, but eternity has the records. So instead of naming individuals on this page and giving them earthly credit, I prefer the Lord Jesus Christ to reward them each as only He can. God bless you all, and may you be surprised as you open up the box that contains your heavenly treasures.

For the Son of man shall come in the glory of his Father with his angels; and then he shall reward every man according to his works (Matthew 16:27).

Introduction

EXPOSING SATAN'S DEVICES is a spiritual tool chest of the many devices Satan uses to keep people under his lies and deceptions which eventually destroys them. It's very broad and yet specific in it's coverage of exposing Satan's devices. Some of the topics covered deal with things we all face in our day with the devil on the rampage.

As long as Satan stays covered he is able to continue his evil works, but when the light of God's Word shines on his deeds, he can no longer use his deceptions. We certainly don't want to allow the devil to get an advantage over us by our ignorance of the devices he uses (**2 Corin. 2:11**).

EXPOSING SATAN'S DEVICES is an expose of Satan and his methods and how to overcome him through spiritual warfare. As overcomers we have the victory!

1

Satan's Description and Deeds

Who Is Satan?

2 Corinthians 2:11 says **Lest Satan should get an advantage of us: for we are not ignorant of his devices**.

Before we discuss some of the devices of Satan, we first need to know who he is. The name Satan comes from a Hebrew word signifying an adversary, an enemy, and an accuser. In God's Word, we discover that Satan is God's enemy and is against all for which God stands. He is the archenemy of good.

Surprising as it may seem to some, Satan was not always evil. In the beginning, he was an angel created in perfection and beauty. Angels were given a will with a free moral choice, and Lucifer (Satan's name before he was cast out of heaven) chose to do evil and rebelled against God. He was cast out of heaven to the earth because of his sin. His present domain is limited to the earth and hell.

Isaiah 14:12-15, How art thou fallen from heaven, O Lucifer, son of the morning! how art thou cut down to the ground, which didst weaken the nations! For thou hast said in thine heart, I will ascend into heaven, I will exalt my throne above the stars of God: I will sit also upon the mount of the congregation, in the sides of the north: I will ascend above the heights of the clouds; I will be like the most High. Yet thou shalt be brought down to hell, to the sides of the pit.

Satan's sins were pride and covetousness. He desired God's throne and set his will against God's will. Five times he said, "I will" in this portion of Scripture.

This is still man's sin today: the refusal to do God's will, with the same attitude of "I will." Satan chose to rebel and it brought

1

him down to hell. Men are making the same choice today and those who rebel will ultimately go down to the pit with the devil.

Lucifer had been gifted with beauty and had walked upon the holy mountain of God. But even with all this, he was not content with his position and by trying to usurp God's authority, sin entered into him when he attempted to overthrow God's kingdom.

Ezekiel 28:12-19, ...Thus saith the Lord God; Thou sealest up the sum, full of wisdom, and perfect in beauty. Thou hast been in Eden the garden of God; every precious stone was thy covering, the sardius, topaz, and the diamond, the beryl, the onyx, and the jasper, the sapphire, the emerald, and the carbuncle, and gold: the workmanship of thy tabrets and of thy pipes was prepared in thee in the day that thou wast created. Thou art the anointed cherub that covereth; and I have set thee so: thou wast upon the holy mountain of God; thou hast walked up and down in the midst of the stones of fire. Thou wast perfect in thy ways from the day that thou wast created, till iniquity was found in thee. By the multitude of thy merchandise they have filled the midst of thee with violence, and thou hast sinned: therefore I will cast thee as profane out of the mountain of God: and I will destroy thee, O covering cherub, from the midst of the stones of fire. Thine heart was lifted up because of thy beauty, thou hast corrupted thy wisdom by reason of thy brightness: I will cast thee to the ground, I will lay thee before kings, that they may behold thee. Thou hast defiled thy sanctuaries by the multitude of thine iniquities, by the iniquity of thy traffick; therefore will I bring forth a fire from the midst of thee, it shall devour thee, and I will bring thee to ashes upon the earth in the sight of all them that behold thee. All they that know thee among the people shall be astonished at thee: thou shalt be a terror, and never shalt thou be any more.

From these verses, we see that God did not create Lucifer

evil, but made him perfect. By Satan's own choice, he became evil and was cast out of heaven.

Satan Cast Out of Heaven

The Lord never meant for evil to exist. It was simply the opposite of good, and since it takes a free will for evil to come into existence, Lucifer was the first created being to exercise his will against God. Since that time, others have followed. Satan caused a third of heaven to fall with him by influencing other angelic beings to make war against God (**Revelation 12:4a**). They too were cast out of heaven. They have since become evil spirits due to their choice. They now roam the earth, with Satan as their leader and master. These invisible supernatural beings still have power, but it is directed toward evil works of darkness.

Satan is still ruling in the earth today, not only over the evil spirits, but also over evil men who choose the same path of rebellion against God. He is the dark prince of this world. We can see a glimpse of his evil wisdom, strength, glitter, and his inevitable end by reading the previous passages. We must remember that he has only limited power, but nevertheless he does have power, and those who do not know him and his devices inevitably become his victims.

Jesus Defeats Satan

Those who are "born again" and filled with the Spirit of God have no need to fear this evil foe as he has been defeated by our God. Jesus defeated him and stripped him of his power two thousand years ago. Jesus paid the price of our sins on the cross and then rose from the dead bringing life to all who would follow Him. Satan's authority has been taken away from him. We now have authority over him through Jesus Christ. **I am he that liveth,** and was dead; and, behold, I am alive for evermore, Amen; and have the keys of hell and of death (Revelation 1:18).

Revelation 12 records the account of Satan's overthrow by Christ. We are first given a vision of what takes place in heaven, then the Bible reveals the earthly scene: **Revelation 12:7-12, And there was war in heaven: Michael and his angels fought against the dragon; and the dragon fought and his angels, And prevailed not; neither was their place found any more in heaven. And the great dragon was cast out, that old serpent, called the Devil, and Satan, which deceiveth the whole world: he was cast out into the earth, and his angels were cast out with him. And I heard a loud voice saying in heaven, Now is come salvation, and strength, and the kingdom of our God, and the power of his Christ: for the accuser of our brethren is cast down, which accused them before our God day and night. And they overcame him by the blood of the Lamb, and by the word of their testimony; and they loved not their lives unto the death. Therefore rejoice, ye heavens, and ye that dwell in them. Woe to the inhabiters of the earth and of the sea! for the devil is come down unto you, having great wrath, because he knoweth that he hath but a short time.**

We Have Power Over the Devil

Although Satan has only a short time, he is doing great damage in the earth today. He particularly has stepped up his work due to the nearness of the Lord's return. He knows that at that time the Bible says he will be cast out of the earth, just as he was cast out of heaven.

We have no reason ever to fear the devil when we belong to God and are walking in His will. In fact, we have been given authority over Satan and all his devils.

Luke 10:17-20, And the seventy returned again with joy, saying, Lord, even the devils are subject unto us through thy

name. **And he said unto them, I beheld Satan as lightning fall from heaven. Behold, I give unto you power to tread on serpents and scorpions, and over all the power of the enemy: and nothing shall by any means hurt you. Notwithstanding in this rejoice not, that the spirits are subject unto you; but rather rejoice, because your names are written in heaven**.

Many of God's people suffer needlessly under Satan's oppression and evil works because they have not been taught their authority in Christ. In the name of Jesus, we can cast out demons and set the captives free (**Mark 16:17-18**). The Lord told us that nothing could harm us and that all power over the devil would be ours.

Should We Ignore Satan?

Many people say they don't want to talk about the devil so as not to bring any glory to him. However, the Bible does not teach that we are to ignore the devil so he will flee, but rather we are to resist the devil so he will flee (**James 4:7**).

How are we to resist the devil? We resist him by using the Word of God against him. We must talk about the devil if we are to understand how to overcome him and expose his evil ways. We cannot defeat an enemy we ignore. The way in which people talk about the devil is what causes an imbalance. If it produces fear, it is not the Lord.

Being overly demon-conscious can cause fear. Some people get so devil-conscious, they begin seeing demons in everyone and everything. This is an extreme that should be avoided. Yet we should not go to the other extreme which totally denies the existence of the devil, demons and eternal hell.

In fact, this extreme is one of Satan's favorite devices: the belief that he and his horde of demons do not exist. He would like for us to believe that he is just a myth (a silly-looking man in a red costume with a long tail). However, he is very real, and one look around will show us the works he is responsible for: the drug scene, violence, sickness, sexual perversion, broken homes, hatred among races, witchcraft, sin and division within the body of Christ. Satan tries to escape the blame for his evil deeds by whispering lies to people, such as, "This problem only happened because you live in the world and these things are just part of this world. As long as you are here you are going to have to put up with sickness, turmoil etc." However, God says: **These things I have spoken unto you, that in me ye might have peace. In the world ye shall have tribulation: but be of good cheer; I have overcome the world (John 16:33).** We do not have to put up with Satan's evil attacks against us and our loved ones; through prayer we can overcome him just as Jesus overcame.

Satan Blames God

Another device of the devil is to blame God for our problems. Satan sends accidents, tragedies, illnesses and financial crises, then tries to convince us that God is chastising us for some wrong. This evil lie of the enemy defames our precious Father Who loves us so much He sent His only Son to die for our sins. If He was willing to do this, giving up His most priceless possession for us, would He then put horrible things on us, while denying us good things? No, our God came to redeem us from the curse, not to put one on us. Satan is the troublemaker, the robber, the thief and the master liar. Jesus, while on earth, went around doing good, healing the sick, setting the captives free and ministering the message of love. The truth is that God chastises us through His Word. When we do wrong, our spirits are chastised and the Lord speaks to us about our wrong. **(Hebrews 12:5, And ye have forgotten the exhortation which speaketh unto you as unto children, My son, despise not thou the chastening of the Lord, nor faint when thou art rebuked of him.)**

We must see the root of our problems is sin and the devil

influences us to sin thus creating our problems. Jesus died to deliver us from sin and the ensuing problems created by that sin.

Two Powers in the Earth

We need to see the true nature of God. By knowing God's attributes we can see the extreme contrast of Satan's nature vs. God's nature. Satan is diametrically opposed to all for which God stands. We need to understand that there are only two supernatural powers in the earth today, and that we are going to be influenced by either one or the other. We cannot remain neutral. The two powers are actually two opposite laws that are working in the world: "the law of life in Christ" and "the law of sin and death" ruled by Satan. **(Romans 8:2, For the law of the Spirit of life in Christ Jesus hath made me free from the law of sin and death.)**

Satan's Servants

Many people are serving Satan out of ignorance, not realizing that they are his victims and pawns. **(Ephesians 4:18, Having the understanding darkened, being alienated from the life of God through the ignorance that is in them, because of the blindness of their heart.)** Others have deliberately chosen to follow the devil.

Romans 1:29-32, Being filled with all unrighteousness, fornication, wickedness, covetousness, maliciousness; full of envy, murder, debate, deceit, malignity; whisperers, Backbiters, haters of God, despiteful, proud, boasters, inventors of evil things, disobedient to parents, Without understanding, covenant-breakers, without natural affection, implacable, unmerciful: Who knowing the judgment of God, that they which commit such things are worthy of death, not only do the same, but have pleasure in them that do them.

Some have chosen to follow their own ways and are thus following the devil because selfishness is part of his nature.

II Timothy 3:2, For men shall be lovers of their own selves, covetous, boasters, proud, blasphemers, disobedient to parents, unthankful, unholy, Without natural affection, trucebreakers, false accusers, incontinent, fierce, despisers of those that are good, Traitors, heady, high-minded, lovers of pleasures more than lovers of God.

And, still others have utterly rejected Christ and therefore are also followers of Satan. **(Mark 16:16, ...He that believeth not shall be damned.)**

Let us look at the nature of Satan so that we will be able to recognize his devices. His lies can be exposed by examining their source, thus perceiving that his work is behind them. Once they are exposed, we can resist the devil and overcome him. It is very important to know the nature and the tactics of our enemy if we are to defeat him.

Exposing Satan's Lies

We read in **Revelation 12:9** the following description of the devil: **And the great dragon was cast out, that old serpent, called the Devil, and Satan, which deceiveth the whole world: he was cast out into the earth, and his angels were cast out with him.** From this, we see that one of Satan's major roles is that of deceiver. He has deceived the whole world. When we are "born again" into the Lord's kingdom, we are no longer a part of this world. If we seek only the Lord for truth, we will no longer remain under bondage to the devil's lies and deception. **(Colossians 1:13, Who hath delivered us from the power of darkness, and hath translated us into the kingdom of his dear Son.)** The only power Satan has over any child of God is the power of deception, and that can be overcome by seeking the Lord and the truth of His Word. Actually, Satan has no power over Christians except what

8

they allow him to have. On the other hand, people in the world who are unbelievers have no protection against the devil and his evils. The only thing that keeps them from immediate death is God's mercy and grace. God is not willing that any should perish. **(II Peter 3:9, The Lord is not slack concerning his promise, as some men count slackness; but is longsuffering to usward, not willing that any should perish, but that all should come to repentance.)**

In Genesis, we find the first account of Satan's deception as he, in the form of a serpent, beguiles the first man and woman that the Lord created. **Genesis 1 and 2** record the creation of the earth and God's special creation, man. **Genesis 1:26-28a reads, And God said, Let us make man in our image, after our likeness: and let them have dominion over the fish of the sea, and over the fowl of the air, and over the cattle, and over all the earth, and over every creeping thing that creepeth upon the earth. So God created man in his own image, in the image of God created he him; male and female created he them. And God blessed them...** As we look at this tragic story, we will discover that the same lies Satan told Adam and Eve are the same ones he is still using today to get man to sin and break fellowship with God. He has not changed his method of attack. By studying **Genesis 1**, we can understand and benefit greatly from the record of the invasion of the planet earth by this hostile power, seeing him strike at God through the ones whom He created and loved. There was a sweet fellowship existing between man and God in the garden of Eden. Satan knew if he could only break the bonds of that fellowship and cause those two in the garden to step out into independence as he had done, then God would lose something which was most precious to Him.

Eve Believes a Lie

Let us notice the serpent's (Satan's) method of deceiving

man. He first came to Eve very subtly, challenging God's instructions to Adam and her. **Genesis 3:1-6** reads, **Now the serpent was more subtle than any beast of the field which the Lord God had made. And he said unto the woman, Yea, hath God said, Ye shall not eat of every tree of the garden? And the woman said unto the serpent, We may eat of the fruit of the trees of the garden: But of the fruit of the tree which is in the midst of the garden, God hath said, Ye shall not eat of it, neither shall ye touch it, lest ye die. And the serpent said unto the woman, Ye shall not surely die: For God doth know that in the day ye eat thereof, then your eyes shall be opened, and ye shall be as gods, knowing good and evil. And when the woman saw that the tree was good for food, and that it was pleasant to the eyes, and a tree to be desired to make one wise, she took of the fruit thereof, and did eat, and gave also unto her husband with her; and he did eat**.

We observe from this account that Satan's first method is to bring doubt against God's judgment by questioning His limits on man. "Hath God said?...God hath said." Then the serpent places three temptations before them: the lust of the flesh, the lust of the eyes and the pride of life. **(1 John 2:16, For all that is in the world, the lust of the flesh, and the lust of the eyes, and the pride of life, is not of the Father, but is of the world.)**

The things of this world still tempt man today. The Greek word used for "world" in the Scriptures is "kosmos." In a study of the Scriptures, we find it used mainly in four ways. First, it is used with reference to the material universe, the world; this earth as seen in **Matthew 13:35, John 1:10,** and **Mark 16:15**.

The second use of the Greek word "kosmos," or world, is for the inhabitants, or men of the world as seen in **John 3:16** and other Scriptures where the idea of the whole race of man is implicated. A third definition for "world" is for "this age" as found in **Matthew 13:39**.

The fourth definition for "world," as used in **1 John 2:16** (this is the world we are told not to love that is under Satan's domain), is the "kosmos" of the moral and spiritual systems we call human society. Fallen society is that realm of the world which consists of the whole circle of worldly goods, endowments, riches, advantages, pleasures, intellectual pursuits, education, science, man-made religious systems, business, medicine, arts and politics. It is this definition of "kosmos" that the Word of God is speaking of as that which is controlled by Satan.

Many of us do not realize that when we touch the things that make up fallen society, we touch the power of Satan. Therefore, we become "independent" in the way we use them if we do not put them under the power and direction of God.

God had not intended to deny man access to the tree of the knowledge of good and evil but had a plan that in time would have opened his eyes to good and evil, and then finally allowed him to partake of the tree of life when he had matured enough to be able to live eternally in that state. By eating the fruit prematurely, it brought death instead of wisdom and life, just as God had told them it would.

Spiritual Death

Physical death did not come immediately, but spiritual death did. They died on the inside first. They no longer could face God. We experience the same feeling when we sin. Fear and shame are the fruits of sin. Many fear God today because of the sin in their lives. If we really fellowship with God on a daily basis, we find that as we obey Him there is simply no guilt or fear that troubles us. However when we sin without repentance, we run from the presence of God just as Adam and Eve did.

Genesis 3:7-14, And the eyes of them both were opened, and they knew that they were naked; and they sewed fig leaves together, and made themselves aprons. And they heard the voice of the Lord God walking in the garden in the cool of the day: and Adam and his wife hid themselves from the pres-

ence of the Lord God amongst the trees of the garden. And the Lord God called unto Adam, and said unto him, Where art thou? And he said, I heard thy voice in the garden, and I was afraid, because I was naked; and I hid myself. And he said, Who told thee that thou wast naked? Hast thou eaten of the tree, whereof I commanded thee that thou shouldest not eat? And the man said, The woman whom thou gavest to be with me, she gave me of the tree, and I did eat. And the Lord God said unto the woman, What is this that thou hast done? And the woman said, The serpent beguiled me, and I did eat. And the Lord God said unto the serpent, Because thou hast done this, thou art cursed above all cattle, and above every beast of the field; upon thy belly shalt thou go, and dust shalt thou eat all the days of thy life.

We see Adam and Eve not only experiencing fear and shame, but also we see another sin rising in Adam's nature as he tries to justify his failure to obey. He blames God for giving him the woman who led him astray. He neither takes responsibility for his own sin nor for the protection of the woman.

Today, we are guilty of the same thing as we often find ourselves blaming God for our failures and disobedience or blaming the people around us. The real problem lies within us. God has a perfect plan for every person, but so many are not willing to walk in that plan. Our society is so eager to get everything immediately that most people fail to wait for God to work out His plan.

Penalties for Sin

God's plan for Adam and Eve was a perfect plan, however their disobedience altered God's original plan for them. They were denied the right to the tree of life while on earth. They were also given penalties for their rebellion.

Genesis 3:16-19, Unto the woman he said, I will greatly multiply thy sorrow and thy conception; in sorrow thou shalt

bring forth children; and thy desire shall be to thy husband, and he shall rule over thee. And unto Adam he said, Because thou hast hearkened unto the voice of thy wife, and hast eaten of the tree, of which I commanded thee, saying, Thou shalt not eat of it: cursed is the ground for thy sake; in sorrow shalt thou eat of it all the days of thy life; Thorns also and thistles shall it bring forth to thee; and thou shalt eat the herb of the field; In the sweat of thy face shalt thou eat bread, till thou return unto the ground; for out of it wast thou taken: for dust thou art, and unto dust shalt thou return.

Genesis 3:23-24, Therefore the Lord God sent him forth from the garden of Eden, to till the ground from whence he was taken. So he drove out the man; and he placed at the east of the garden of Eden Cherubims, and a flaming sword which turned every way, to keep the way of the tree of life.

Satan cared nothing for the suffering that would follow after man's disobedience. All he wished to accomplish was a breakdown in the holy communion between God and His children. This was his objective then, and it is still his basic objective today. He deceives and motivates Christians to step out independently thus destroying their faith in God.

Satan's Way Is Selfishness

Man yields to the devil by going his own selfish way. Satan's nature is characterized by exhalting "self" through fleshly will power. This is exactly what "humanism" is. Man seeks to be independent of the power of God. Thus the sins of pride, lust, greed, covetousness, and all other "self" interests are part of Satan's nature. The nature of God is love. Love is characterized by giving all. (John 3:16, For God so loved the world, that he gave his only begotten Son, that whosoever believeth in him should not perish, but have everlasting life.)

We are taught in the Scriptures to "deny self." This means

13

we are to disown, or refuse to acknowledge our "self will power," which seeks only for "self." We are to give all of our being to God and love Him with all of our heart, mind, body, strength, and soul. The degree to which we worship or serve "self" reflects the degree to which we are yielding to the spirit of Satan. He is a deceiver and epitomizes self-seeking.

Let us look at another aspect of his work as deceiver. After we have come to the Lord and committed our lives totally to God, we no longer wish to displease Him, so we flee from the obvious works of darkness. The devil then ceases to come to us with the usual temptations because we have learned to resist and not yield to him in those areas. He must now come in another way to get us to believe that what he proposes is God's will for us; otherwise we would rebuke him. He comes imitating the Holy Spirit, attempting to make us receive his plan instead of God's plan for our lives.

Evil Can Be Turned to Good

Many of us have been deceived in this area and have taken steps we later have discovered were the result of deception by the enemy. We thought we were doing the will of God, but found we had been misled. Eve was innocently deceived by the serpent, but then by God's grace, He promised that through her seed would come the defeat of the one who had deceived her. **(Genesis 3:15, And I will put enmity between thee and the woman, and between thy seed and her seed; it shall bruise thy head, and thou shalt bruise his heel.)**

Yes, God can turn the very devices of the enemy into weapons of victory over him! Willful transgression brings the judgment of God upon it, even though the transgressor can be forgiven. Moreover, every single thing in which Satan may have deceived us as innocent victims of his wiles can become the very cause of his defeat.

God gives comfort to those who have been fooled by Satan. This is especially true for those of God's children who have been deceived by "supernatural manifestations" which afterwards were found not to be of God, and to those who have fallen into depression, darkness and despair. We can rise from despair by asking God to turn what Satan has meant for evil into good for our lives and for all those involved. **Genesis 50:20** states, **But as for you, ye thought evil against me; but God meant it unto good, to bring to pass, as it is this day, to save much people alive.**

Pride and Beauty a Snare

Pride is another one of Satan's attributes. This pride is directed towards his own beauty and accomplishments; **Ezekiel 28:17** points this out: **Thine heart was lifted up because of thy beauty, thou hast corrupted thy wisdom by reason of thy brightness: I will cast thee to the ground, I will lay thee before kings, that they may behold thee.** Many today are afflicted with this same pride. Those in the world are seeking beauty today as never before. Beauty aids, makeup, glamorous clothes, beautiful homes and plush automobiles are only a few of the things the world is seeking today. These things in themselves are not evil, but the lust for them is. **(1 John 2:16, For all that is in the world, the lust of the flesh, and the lust of the eyes, and the pride of life, is not of the Father, but is of the world.)** Satan's unusual beauty was one of the causes of his destruction. It contributed to the excessive development of his pride.

Spiritual beauty is also a deadly trap. God blesses many with His gifts and graces, but then those same gifts become a source of pride when the people cease to be able to handle them with humility. They begin seeing themselves as better than others and soon take credit for their holiness and spirituality instead of glorifying God. This ultimately leads to their fall. **(Proverbs 16:18, Pride goeth before destruction, and an haughty spirit before a fall.)**

Many refuse to give their gifts back to God because they love to be seen exhibiting them and using them to manipulate others. If they persist in refusing to surrender them, the Holy Spirit will eventually depart, and Satan will gladly replace God's gifts with his false gifts. The change can be so subtle that the person does not even recognize Satan's take over. In fact, many think they have received greater gifts. The big difference from this point on, however, is that their gifts no longer stress fellowship with the Lord, nor cause souls to repent, nor stimulate joy and peace in the Lord. The false gifts that have been substituted will only excite the flesh.

Examples of this would be prophecies that promote pride in others, words of knowledge that deal with only the things of this world (houses, cars, lands, business deals, etc.), or words that promote giving to their ministries. Even casting out devils and doing wonderful works can be done by those whose hearts are not right with God.

Matthew 7:22-23 says, **...Lord, Lord, have we not prophesied in thy name? and in thy name have cast out devils? and in thy name done many wonderful works? And then will I profess unto them, I never knew you: depart from me, ye that work iniquity.**

The Devil Is a Liar

Another description that identifies the devil is that of a wolf in sheep's clothing. The motive of the wolf is to steal, plunder, and destroy.

The Lord describes Satan as just that kind of character. The Pharisees were attempting to discount Jesus' ministry by boasting of Abraham as their father. Jesus went to the very heart of their allegiance in **John 8:44** when he said, **Ye are of your father the devil, and the lusts of your father ye will do. He was a murderer from the beginning, and abode not in the truth, be-**

1 6

cause there is no truth in him. When he speaketh a lie, he speaketh of his own: for he is a liar, and the father of it.

The devil is a liar, a thief and a murderer. **John 10:10** says, **The thief cometh not, but for to steal, and to kill, and to destroy: I am come that they might have life, and that they might have it more abundantly**.

Rebuke the Devil

Satan is described by Jesus as the robber and the thief. We must be reminded of this and protect those things God has given us from his devices. When we receive anything from the Lord, Satan stands ready to rob us of it.

When we are saved, Satan immediately tries to convince us we really aren't saved, or if we receive a healing from God he will try to talk us out of it. We may go for a month or longer without a symptom from whatever we were healed of, and then Satan will give us a symptom again to try and convince us that we have lost what the Lord has given us. We must learn to stand on God's Word, not our feelings in the matter, as we can be robbed of our inheritance if we do not continue to stand against the enemy's lies. We are to rebuke the devil and claim the promises of healing. By trusting and believing God, we will find our health and peace of mind restored. This is the manner in which we should deal with the devil when he comes to rob what the Lord has given us.

If we have never received our healing to begin with, we need to seek God and fellowship with Him until we come to that place where we are able to receive His healing. To rebuke symptoms when we have not yet received a healing is futile, as we need to be delivered from the root cause of our sickness before the sickness will leave permanently. We can find this root cause by seeking God with our whole heart and by laying down our lives before Him to use as He desires.

Overcoming Satan's Lies

Not only is the devil a robber and thief, but a master liar. He is always attacking the truth of God's Word. The people who fall for his lies are those that do not know God's Word. Satan has no new lies, just new victims. The victims are the people who believe him. There are no temptations that others have not also experienced.

There hath no temptation taken you but such as is common to man: but God is faithful, who will not suffer you to be tempted above that ye are able; but will with the temptation also make a way to escape, that ye may be able to bear it (I Corinthians 10:13).

We must continually ask God to reveal Satan's lies and temptations to us so that we may overcome him.

Jesus wants to give us abundant life, while Satan seeks to destroy. We must be on guard so as not to be fooled by him because he does not come announcing himself as the devil, but instead appears as a sheep rather than a wolf. **Matthew 7:15** says, **Beware of false prophets, which come to you in sheep's clothing, but inwardly they are ravening wolves.** We must seek God for discernment so that we will not be fooled by outward appearances.

Satan often poses as the Holy Spirit and speaks to us as if he were God. **1 Peter 5:8, Be sober, be vigilant; because your adversary the devil, as a roaring lion, walketh about, seeking whom he may devour.** In this verse, we see the devil comes as a roaring lion. Jesus is referred to in Scripture as the Lion of Judah. **(Revelation 5:5, And one of the elders saith unto me, Weep not: behold, the Lion of the tribe of Judah, the Root of David, hath prevailed to open the book, and to loose the seven seals thereof.)** Because Satan imitates the Lord Jesus (trying to be like the real Lion of Judah); we are told to watch, beware, and be vigilant because Satan is the lion that seeks to devour.

Don't Ignore the Devil

We are not to ignore the devil, but rather to look out for him. As we have mentioned previously, some people get very upset when the subjects of Satan, evil and hell are discussed. They declare that they do not want to talk about the devil. However, the Word of God has much to say on these subjects. In fact, the words Satan, devil, Lucifer, and hell are mentioned over 980 times. The Lord was not silent on these subjects, but rather gave us warnings so we would be prepared for Satan's attacks, as well as to know the ways in which we are to overcome him and thereby escape hell. The devil is seeking those whom he may devour, and he finds many easy victims because they do not even believe in the reality of his activity nor in the prospect of hell. Satan has darkened the minds of those in the world so that they cannot see the true picture of him and the horrible fate that awaits all who follow him.

Satan appears as an "angel of light" in order to seduce people into following him. He also has disciples even as Jesus had his disciples. **2 Corinthians 11:13-15, For such are false apostles, deceitful workers, transforming themselves into the apostles of Christ. And no marvel; for Satan himself is transformed into an angel of light. Therefore it is no great thing if his ministers also be transformed as the ministers of righteousness; whose end shall be according to their works.**

We must look at the works of men to discern which god they are serving, the god of this world, Satan, or the true and living God. We are not to look to gifts of preaching, prophecy, material possessions, nor the number of their followers. What kind of works are they producing? Works of the flesh or works of the Spirit? What fruit is evident in their lives? We must be able to recognize our enemy to be able to overcome him. We are in a spiritual war and we cannot fight an enemy we do not know.

In military strategy, one of the enemy's devices is to camouflage its troops so that they cannot be recognized. Satan uses this device also and comes to deceive us, trying to get us to believe that his plan is the best for our lives, rather than the Lord's.

We must be sure that any message we receive agrees with the Word of God. If it does not, we should throw it out. We must be sure our own hearts are right with the Lord, for a clean and pure heart will keep us in the right path. **(Psalm 119:1, Blessed are the undefiled in the way, who walk in the law of the Lord.)** God's will for us will bring peace and rest to our spirit, not anxiety and restlessness. Satan's way is a way of unrest and worry. **(Isaiah 57:20-21, But the wicked are like the troubled sea, when it cannot rest, whose waters cast up mire and dirt. There is no peace, saith my God, to the wicked.)**

The Holy Spirit is gentle and patient, not pushy or rude. We should be wary of any message that would prompt us to react hastily or rashly.

After we check each of these things and still have a deep peace in our spirits regarding a needed action on our part, then we can move ahead in faith and trust the Father to keep us in whatever decision we make. He will protect us and not allow us to be overcome by the devil.

1 John 4:4 says, **Ye are of God, little children, and have overcome them: because greater is he that is in you, than he (Satan) that is in the world.**

Satan Is a False Light

Satan is an angel of false light. He certainly has glitter and glamour, but his fire turns to ashes. The Bible tells us that those who refuse to be taken in by Satan's false light will one day be able to see him for what he is.

Isaiah 14:16, They that see thee shall narrowly look upon thee, and consider thee, saying, Is this the man that made the earth to tremble, that did shake kingdoms; That made the world as a wilderness, and destroyed the cities thereof; that opened not the house of his prisoners?

Isaiah 14:12, How art thou fallen from heaven, O Lucifer, son of the morning! how art thou cut down to the ground, which didst weaken the nations.

The name Lucifer comes from the Latin words "lux" (light) and "ferre" (to bear). He originally was a light bearer; since being cast from heaven, he is now only the bearer of false or "black" light. He is the prince of darkness and much of his evil work goes on in dark places. He also attacks the dark places of our knowledge of God, and since we do not have God's light in those areas, he is able to do his work of deception.

The Hebrew word for Lucifer is "heylel." If we look at the root word of "heylel" we find that it is a false light or the false son of the morning. Jesus is the true morning star. The root of "heylel" is the word "halal" and its varied meanings give us a description of Satan: "to shine; hence to make show, to boast; and thus to be clamorously foolish; to rave; to celebrate; also to stultify: (make) boast (self), celebrate, deal, make foolish, glory, to give light, be (make, feign self) mad (against), etc." (Definition taken from Strong's Concordance). Glittering Lucifer is the old serpent, the devil. Serpents enjoy dark holes, thus we see how darkness is more conducive to Satan's evil ways, like dark nightclubs, bars, and parked cars at night. Most criminals and molesters prowl in the darkness. Witchcraft and seances are practiced in the dark. The Bible says, **And this is the condemnation, that light is come into the world, and men loved darkness rather than light, because their deeds were evil. For every one that doeth evil hateth the light, neither cometh to the light, lest his deeds be reproved. But he that doeth truth cometh to the light, that his deeds may be made manifest, that they are wrought in God (John 3:19-21).**

2

False Religions of Cults and Occults

Satan Loves Religion

Satan, by acting as an angel of light, has tried to devise a spiritual counterfeit for all of God's real workings. Let us examine some of his fakes. One of Satan's favorite frauds is to have a "false religion" preach a "counterfeit gospel." Satan loves religion and has many people practicing false ones all around the world. Many of them even mention Jesus. Satan does not mind even a little truth mixed into false religions as long as The Truth (Jesus) is not taught. In fact, most counterfeit religions have a thread of truth running through them with the devil's lies woven around it. Otherwise Satan could not ensnare people into them. Satan even takes man's craving for the supernatural and creates religions that perform supernatural feats. Many precious Christians have been deceived and become totally or partially involved with one or more of these religions. Since these religions have their origin from the devil, they produce many needless problems and sicknesses for the person involved because they are forms of idolatry.

Gods and Idols

What is idolatry? It is worship of any god outside of the true and living God. Worship is not confined to prayer in a church service, but is having an intense love or admiration for anything. This includes the reverence of any deity.

Exodus 20:3-6, Thou shalt have no other Gods before me. Thou shalt not make unto thee any graven image, or any likeness of any thing that is in heaven above, or that is in the earth beneath, or that is in the water under the earth: Thou shalt not bow down thyself to them, nor serve them: for I the Lord thy God am a jealous God, visiting the iniquity of the fathers upon the children unto the third and fourth generation of them that hate me; And shewing mercy unto thousands of them that love me, and keep my commandments.

The word "god" has many meanings. Anything which a man considers to be most important in his life, whose power he thinks is the greatest, and whose favor he would do anything or give anything to win, is properly called his "god." A man may have many gods. When a man worships anything other than the God of the Bible, we say he is worshiping an "idol."

An idol may be attractive or ugly. An idol may be a concrete thing, a mythical character, or a mental ideal. But, it is always something a person serves with all he is or has. Some people worship drink, pleasure, money, power and even other people. Whatever or whomever I put first in my heart is god to me. Sometimes a person will worship himself. He can do this by living for himself and doing only the things which please him. This is in essence the religion of "Humanism". **Colossians 3:5** says, **Mortify therefore your members which are upon the earth; fornication, uncleanness, inordinate affection, evil concupiscence, and covetousness, which is idolatry**. We are to have no other gods before the true and living God. When Christians speak of God, they mean the God of Abraham, Isaac and Jacob -- the God and Father of our Lord Jesus Christ, the God of the Bible.

False Religions

False religions do not preach the true gospel message which includes the atoning blood of Jesus, His second coming to this earth, a literal fiery hell that is eternal, and the one way to heaven through Jesus Christ alone. False religions show us many paths to heaven and subsequent escape from eternal hell, or they discount hell altogether. Let us look at some of the well-known false religions which are classified as cults. Remember that a cult has threads of truth from the Bible, but is in gross error in one or more of the basic Bible doctrines. Some churches have entered into cultic practices because they have embraced doctrines that either "add to" or "take away" from the Word of God. Some have a greater percentage of error than others, but any degree of error leads to God's disapproval.

Deuteronomy 12:32, What thing soever I command you, observe to do it: thou shalt not add thereto, nor diminish from it.

Revelation 22:18-19, For I testify unto every man that heareth the words of the prophecy of this book, If any man shall add unto these things, God shall add unto him the plagues that are written in this book: And if any man shall take away from the words of the book of this prophecy, God shall take away his part out of the book of life, and out of the holy city, and from the things which are written in this book.

Cults and False Religious Movements
Anglo-Israelism
Armstrong's Worldwide Church of God
Baha-ism
Buddhism
Christian Science
Concept Therapy
Confucianism
Eckankar
Freemasons
Hinduism
Holistic Healing
Humanism

I AM
Inner Peace Movement
Islam
Jainism
Jehovah's Witnesses
Judaism
Liberalism
Modernism
Mormonism
Muslim
National Council of Churches
Neo-Orthodoxy
New Age Movement
New Thought
Rosicrucianism
Scientology
Secret Societies
Sikhism
Social Gospel
Spiritual Frontiers Fellowship
Spiritualism
Swedenborgianism
Taoism
Theosophical Society
Ultimate Reconciliation
Unitarianism
Unification Church (Moonies)
Unity School of Christianity
Universalism
World Council of Churches
Zoroastrianism

NOTE: Although some churches are not traditionally known as cults, they embrace cultic practices; thereby much error is present. These churches practice pagan idolatry as they worship statues and exalt other people above Jesus. They also communicate with the dead which is forbidden in the Bible as it is called Necromancy (**Deut. 18:10-12**). Legalism is very prevalent in these churches. Of course, there are those in these groups who have accepted Jesus as their personal Savior and have been "born again"; however, they never can rise to the overcoming life in Christ due to the cultic influences of these churches. There are, of course, many other cults not listed, but the complete list would be endless. These cults represent the earnest attempt of millions of people to fulfill deep and legitimate needs of the human spirit, which many seem not to have found in the established churches. God loves all these people and desires that they come to the knowledge of the truth. (Some people within these groups are Christians as they have found the Lord in spite of the doctrinal errors. The Holy Spirit will always attempt to lead them out from under the bondage these sects have brought them if their hearts are right.) Dr. Walter Martin's *The Kingdom of the Cults* is a very thorough study of cultic doctrines if you desire information about any of these groups.

God's Way Is Narrow

The way of the masses is not the pathway Jesus speaks of in the Bible. **Matthew 7:13-14** says, **Enter ye in at the strait gate: for wide is the gate, and broad is the way, that leadeth to destruction, and many there be which go in thereat: Because strait is the gate, and narrow is the way, which leadeth unto life, and few there be that find it.** Right after this verse the Lord warns us of the false prophets which are ravening wolves who can be recognized by their fruits. Satan seeks to lead men down any path except the one that leads to life in Christ. True religion is not a particular church or denomination, but an attitude of our hearts and a relationship with Jesus Christ. We are the church; our body becomes the temple of the Holy Spirit when we are "born again." The Lord does lead us to fellowship with other members of the body of Christ and those local gatherings have come to be known as the church. However, all believers make up the true church, and the true kingdom is within.

Luke 17:20-21, And when he was demanded of the Pharisees, when the kingdom of God should come, he answered them and said, The kingdom of God cometh not with observation: Neither shall they say, Lo here! or, lo there! for, behold, the kingdom of God is within you.

If we know any people that are involved in any of these cults, we should love them, pray for them, and seek the Lord as to how we can minister the truth to them. We should not condemn them because Satan has them blinded; they need our love and prayers.

Perhaps you have been involved in one of these false religions and did not know it was in error. You can be set free by seeking the Lord and asking for His truth about it, and then asking Him to deliver you from all its spiritual bondage and physical involvement. Should you have questions as to why any of these are false, as well as the particular doctrines that are in error, as we have mentioned Dr. Walter Martin has written an excellent book called *The Kingdom of the Cults* that exposes these cults and their origins. A good check to see if any one of these holds spiritual bondage over your life is to note your reaction while reading the list. Many people become angry when a certain one is mentioned and cannot believe that particular group could be in error. This indicates the need to seek the Lord. (Why the anger if they have the truth?) When we walk in the truth, we do not become angry if someone disagrees with us. We have an inner witness of God's peace when we are walking in the light.

Doctrines of Demons

Occultism is another work of Satan which counterfeits the true worship of God and the gifts of the Spirit. Occultism is the involvement with the hidden or secret works of darkness. Satan is the master ruler of darkness.

Ephesians 6:12, For we wrestle not against flesh and blood, but against principalities, against powers, against the rulers of the darkness of this world, against spiritual wickedness in high places.

The occult practices hidden things of darkness and promotes doctrines of demons. There has never been a time in history when the warnings against the dangers of occultism were more necessary than at the present. There has been a flood of Satan's evil in the last few years as never before. He knows his time is short so he is out to ensnare all that he can. **(I Timothy 4:1, Now the Spirit speaketh expressly, that in the latter times some shall depart from the faith, giving heed to seducing spirits, and doctrines of devils.)**

Multitudes of Christians and non-Christians alike are finding themselves suffering physical, mental, psychic and spiritual oppression, few realizing that it is because they have allowed themselves to become ensnared in the diabolical web of occultism which is under the influence and control of the powers of darkness. We are going to list only those occult practices that are most common as it is impossible to name them all.

Occult and Occult Practices

Acupuncture
Akashic Records
Alchemy
Almanac Predictions
Age of Aquarius & Aquarian Gospel
Astral Projection or Soul Travel
Astrology
Atlantis
Auras
Automatic Writing
Biorhythm

Black Arts
Black Magic
Black Mass
Body Piercings
Channeling
Clairaudience
Clairvoyance
Charms
Devil's Pentagram
Dream Analysis (Outside of God)
Exorcism
Extrasensory Perception (ESP)
Fortune-telling or Divination
Great Seal
Handwriting Analysis or Graphology
Horoscopes
Hypnosis
I Ching
Incubus and Succubus Demon Man-
ifestations
Kabala
Levitation
Martial Arts
Materializations
Mediums, Psychics
Metaphysics
Numerology (False)
Palmistry
Pendulum Healing
Phrenology
Person Programming
Psychic Portrait
Pyramidology
Reincarnation
Satanism
Satanic Bible
Seances   29

Sorcery
Superstition
Table-Tipping
Talismans
Tarot cards
Tatoos
Tea Leaves
Telepathy
Transcendental Meditation (TM)
Witchcraft & Fetishes
Unidentified Flying Objects (UFO's)
Voodoo
Water Divining or Water Witching
White Magic
Yoga
Zodiac Studies

Damnable Heresies

It would take an overly extensive volume to cover all the
Scriptures that reveal errors in each of the cults and the occult
groups individually, so we cannot pursue that study here. However, there are certain characteristics and marks that identify their
practices. If we are aware of these, we can avoid being led astray
and also help others to see the error. Cults and the occult are
religious perversions and are spoken of as heresies in the Bible.

**But there were false prophets also among the people, even
as there shall be false teachers among you, who privily shall
bring in damnable heresies, even denying the Lord that
brought them, and bring upon themselves swift destruction.
And many shall follow their pernicious ways; by reason of
whom the way of truth shall be evil spoken of. And through
convetousness shall they with feigned words make merchan-**

dise of you: whose judgment now of a long time lingereth not, and their damnation slumbereth not (II Peter 2:1-3).

From a portion of this passage, **denying the Lord that bought them**, we can see that one of the first signs of a false religion is that its followers deny the Lord Jesus as Saviour of the world. It is clear then that the test of a true representative of the Gospel has to do with the definition of the person and the work of Jesus Christ.

Jesus the God-Man

The central truth of Christianity is the doctrine and the nature of the person of Jesus Christ. Christianity always affirms the true deity and the true humanity of our blessed Saviour. He is both fully God and fully man, being the true union of the two natures. Denial of Christ's atoning work on the cross is another heresy accepted by those that are false. They discount the blood shed by Jesus on the cross and become "bloodless religions," speaking of Jesus as a good man or a prophet of God, but denying Him as the Son of God. They also deny the virgin birth, His bodily resurrection and or discount His second return to the earth. The Holy Trinity of God is rejected by many of the cults.

The question "What think ye of Jesus?" is answered correctly only by the believing Christian. The Christian gladly answers, "Jesus Christ is the only begotten Son of the living God, God incarnate in the form of human flesh, born of a virgin. He is the Son of man, the only Saviour of the world, the Author and Finisher of our faith, who, through His death on the cross, provides redemption for all who believe in Him. He is the one who died for our sins, rose again on the third day, who lives to make intercession for us before the Father, and who will one day come in His glorious body, returning to judge the quick and the dead at His appearing in His kingdom. He is Lord and God, and in Him alone we have life, and life more abundantly. Jesus is the Son represented in the Godhead. The only true God is one God, eternally existent in three persons: Father, Son, and Holy Spirit. Each person of the Godhead is eternal and coequal with the others. The Holy Bible is the recorded Word of God and is infallible. It is the final authority in regard to all Christian doctrine. Jesus Christ, our Lord and Saviour, is the central figure of the Bible and we have our life solely in Him."

False views of God and the Saviour make references to them in such terms as "the ideal truth," "the divine idea," "the greatest personage," "the chief agent of life," "the glorious spirit creature," "the unity of all mankind," and "the greatest master teacher." Their terms and definitions of God are vague and confusing. They talk of having "conscious communion with God," "experiencing eternal order by inner sublime peace," and "universal unity coexisting with man's spirit."

Doctrinal Confusion

Doctrinal ambiguity is thus another definite mark of cults. They are never clear in their definitions or explanations and frequently change their beliefs and rules to adapt to their continued doctrinal alterations. When any of their beliefs stem from the Bible, they come from segmented portions of Scripture taken out of context to read as they dictate. Usually a misplaced emphasis on a portion of the Word becomes the test of true religion to them. If others do not accept and believe their doctrine, they are not considered saved.

Cults Are Clannish

Cults are very clannish and look on all others as lost except for those in their group. They cease to base salvation on a person's individual relationship with Christ and extend it only to those who have membership in their group. This membership then brings the people into bondage as they are required generally to follow a certain set of rules in order to be acceptable to God. Many are brought into slavery to their leaders. They must follow their advice and their dictates, for to do otherwise would mean loss of their salvation. Heaven is attained by working to please the leaders of these false religions. Some serve living leaders, while others follow the teachings of a "master" who has written a book considered equal to the Bible. Examples would be the Book of Mormon, the Koran and the Vedas. These leaders are generally people who claim to have had "special revelation."

We find the spirit of pride and self-elevation is always present in these groups. They speak of "my message," "my revelation," "my leadership," and "my people." Their followers become so mesmerized that many become unable to even seek a way out. Others are held in bondage by a spirit of fear and dependency. They would love to be free but are threatened with all kinds of disasters and the fear of going to hell should they depart.

Spirit of Fear

Only through Christ can this spirit of fear and bondage be broken. Fear is never from the Lord, and a good test to see if we are serving the true God is to check and see if we are following out of fear or out of love. **For God hath not given us the spirit of fear; but of power, and of love, and of a sound mind (2 Timothy 1:7).** God leads His followers with respect and love. Satan's false religions enslave through fear and false promises. There is always a "carrot on a stick" which one never does quite get. Uncertainty is another favorite cult weapon. One never knows exactly where he stands or whether he will make heaven or not. Legalism reigns and there are myriad sets of rules that must be followed. If they are violated, certain disaster is prophesied by those in command. Anything that brings a person into bondage is never from the Lord. Jesus came to set us free. **And ye shall know the truth, and the truth shall make you free (John 8:32).** We should flee anything that would bring us into bondage of man or Satan. **Ye are bought with a price; be not ye the servants of men (1 Corinthians 7:23). Where the spirit of the Lord is, there is liberty (2 Corinthians 3:17).**

Hell Is a Reality

Another earmark of cultic religions is their views about hell. If they do not use the fear of going to hell to bring people into bondage, then they try to discount hell altogether.

One of Satan's favorite lies is to try to convince people that they suffer their hell on earth and that there is none hereafter. He also tries to get them to believe the lie that death only brings a state of sleep or rest.

Another doctrine teaches that hell is only temporary and eventually after being in the fires of hell people become cleansed and purified to the degree that they will then be accepted into heaven. These terrible heresies are believed by many Christians who are ignorant of what God's Word has to say about it.

Cults also teach that hell is a place where souls are simply annihilated and therefore no longer exist. Some teach reincarnation, giving people another chance to be born on this earth for as many times as it takes to become purified, progressing to higher forms each time they return. Others say hell is only a place away from God, but it is not a literal burning fiery hell.

What does the Bible say about hell? Jesus described this place as such a place of horror that it would be better to sever a member of our body that would lead us there than to end up in that place of torments.

And if thy hand offend thee, cut it off: it is better for thee to enter into life maimed, than having two hands to go into hell, into the fire that never shall be quenched: Where

their worm dieth not, and the fire is not quenched. And if thy foot offend thee, cut it off: it is better for thee to enter halt into life, than having two feet to be cast into hell, into the fire that never shall be quenched: Where their worm dieth not, and the fire is not quenched. And if thine eye offend thee, pluck it out: it is better for thee to enter into the kingdom of God with one eye, than having two eyes to be cast into hell fire: Where their worm dieth not, and the fire is not quenched (Mark 9:43-48).

We see clearly that His statement signifies the exclusion of the hope of restoration and that the punishment is eternal. He repeats the words, **where their worm dieth not, and the fire is not quenched**, three times for emphasis. Another account of the torments of hell is found in **Luke 16:19-26**:

There was a certain rich man, which was clothed in purple and fine linen, and fared sumptuously every day: And there was a certain beggar named Lazarus, which was laid at his gate, full of sores, And desiring to be fed with the crumbs which fell from the rich man's table: moreover the dogs came and licked his sores. And it came to pass, that the beggar died, and was carried by the angels into Abraham's bosom: the rich man also died, and was buried; And in hell he lift up his eyes, being in torments, and seeth Abraham afar off, and Lazarus in his bosom. And he cried and said, Father Abraham, have mercy on me, and send Lazarus, that he may dip the tip of his finger in water, and cool my tongue; for I am tormented in this flame. But Abraham said, Son, remember that thou in thy lifetime receivedst thy good things, and likewise Lazarus evil things: but now he is comforted, and thou art tormented. And beside all this, between us and you there is a great gulf fixed: so that they which would pass from hence to you cannot; neither can they pass to us, that would come from thence.

Hell is described not only as a fiery place of torment, but also as a separation from God and His saints, a place where there is continual torment.

Hell Made for Satan

This place was prepared for the devil and his fallen angels. It was never meant for man to go there. Man is going there by choosing to follow Satan and his evil ways. **Then shall he say also unto them on the left hand, Depart from me, ye cursed, into everlasting fire, prepared for the devil and his angels: (Matthew 25:41).**

The Greek word for hell in the New Testament, "hades" means the same as "sheol" in the Old Testament Hebrew. It is also spoken of as the grave, the pit, and the place of the dead. It is described as below the surface of the earth (**Numbers 16:30, Psalm 55:15**), beneath the depths of the sea, and is also spoken of as "the deep." It has gates and bars that hold its prisoners. The wicked go down into the region of hell where they are kept in torment until the day of the White Throne Judgment. Hell is a place of shame, remorse, consciousness, memory, and anguish.

Paradise

There was also a region in hell known as "Paradise" where the righteous dead went prior to Calvary. It was separated by a great impassable gulf from the lower regions. It was a place of peace and comfort and was the place referred to as "Abraham's Bosom." Not only was Abraham there, but all the Old Testament saints were kept there until Christ's crucifixion. Christ then descended into hell (sheol, hades) (**Psalm 16:10**) (**Luke 23:43**) and at His ascension He led "captivity captive" and delivered the prisoners of hope from "Paradise" (a compartment in hell) and led them to heaven.

Ephesians 4:8-10 says, **Wherefore he saith, When he ascended up on high, he led captivity captive, and gave gifts unto men. (Now that he ascended, what is it but that he also**

descended first into the lower parts of the earth? He that descended is the same also that ascended up far above all heavens, that he might fill all things.

The gates of hell (sheol and hades) do not prevail against the church today as they once did against the righteous in the Old Testament. All true believers go directly to heaven at death and do not wait in "Paradise" as the Old Testament saints did. (**Matthew 16:18, 2 Corinthians 5:8**).

Lake of Fire

Christ has the keys to death and hell which will ultimately have to give up its wicked dead for judgment. "Sheol" and "hades" (hell) will then come to an end and "Gehenna" (the "Lake of Fire") will take its place. Souls will burn forever there with no escape; this is the second death.

I am he that liveth, and was dead; and, behold, I am alive for evermore, Amen; and have the keys of hell and of death (Revelation 1:18).

And the devil that deceived them was cast into the lake of fire and brimstone, where the beast and the false prophet are, and shall be tormented day and night for ever and ever. And I saw a great white throne, and him that sat on it, From whose face the earth and the heaven fled away; and there was found no place for them. And I saw the dead, small and great, stand before God; and the books were opened: and another book was opened, which is the book of life: and the dead were judged out of those things which were written in the books, according to their works. And the sea gave up the dead which were in it; and death and hell delivered up the dead which were in them: and they were judged every man according to their works. And death and hell were cast into the lake of fire. This is the second death. And whosoever was

not found written in the book of life was cast into the lake of fire (Revelation 20:10-15).

Hell and hellfire are realities according to God's Word and any that speak otherwise are in error and are promoting false doctrine.

Enslaved Followers

The New Testament also emphasizes that Christian leaders are never to dominate the lives of others.

The elders which are among you I exhort, who am also an elder, and a witness of the sufferings of Christ, and also a partaker of the glory that shall be revealed: Feed the flock of God which is among you, taking the oversight thereof, not by constraint, but willingly; not for filthy lucre, but of a ready mind; Neither as being lords over God's heritage, but being ensamples to the flock (1 Peter 5:1-3).

True men of God lead their followers by being an example to them. Money cannot influence them. Cults and the occult have the "love of money" at the root of their religions. **For the love of money is the root of all evil: which while some coveted after, they have erred from the faith, and pierced themselves through with many sorrows (1 Timothy 6:10).**

God's true leaders invite Christians to give gladly out of a full heart, while they conduct their own lives on a plane of personal sacrifice, just as the early Christian leaders did. This is in striking contrast to cultic practitioners of today. They stongly imply that money contributed to the cause will buy privileges, gifts, or powers for the beneficent follower. They offer healing and deliverance from accidents for a price. One can even buy his own salvation for a price. Followers are pressured and exploited to the point of economic exhaustion. There are many accounts of wives and children who have been brought to the point of hunger and impoverishment because of the cultic contributions of their husbands and fathers. Enamored of their new spiritual leader, they forget the clear teaching of the Scripture. **If any provide not for his own, and specially for those of his own house, he hath denied the faith, and is worse than an infidel (1 Timothy 5:8).**

Many false religious leaders have their consciences seared and provide for themselves massive homes, spacious estates, and large holdings in the commercial world while their followers live in want and poverty. **Now the Spirit speaketh expressly, that in the latter times some shall depart from the faith, giving heed to seducing spirits, and doctrines of devils; Speaking lies in hypocrisy; having their conscience seared with a hot iron (1 Timothy 4:1-2).** These evil men enslave their followers not only physically by extracting funds from them, but psychologically and spiritually as well.

False Revelation

Another "red flag" to watch for as a sign of the false cults is the promise of a "secret revelation" to the members of their group. Many secret societies give information and privileges to only those within who are promised spiritual advancement not attainable by others. Any time something is presented as "secret," "special" or "the hidden mystery" for only a few (those few who join them), we can deduce that it is not of the Lord. Jesus came with His teachings and message of salvation for all. Witchcraft in the United States is prospering because of leaders who claim to have discovered the "secrets" of prosperity, health, victory over our environment or some other quest or desire. People willingly flock around the religious leader who has "discovered the secret" and is willing to pass it on to them, of course for a price. Jesus warned us of these people.

For there shall arise false Christs, and false prophets, and shall shew great signs and wonders; insomuch that, if it were possible, they shall deceive the very elect. Behold, I have

told you before. Wherefore if they shall say unto you, Behold, he is in the desert; go not forth; behold, he is in the secret chambers; believe it not (Matthew 24:24-26).

Revelation of Mysteries

Most people do not know that all hidden mysteries are to be revealed to those who follow Christ and are given freely without cost.

And he said unto them, Unto you it is given to know the mystery of the kingdom of God... (Mark 4:11).

Now to him that is of power to stablish you according to my gospel, and the preaching of Jesus Christ, according to the revelation of the mystery, which was kept secret since the world began, But now is made manifest, and by the Scriptures of the prophets, according to the commandment of the everlasting God, made known to all nations for the obedience of faith (Romans 16:25-26).

Nevertheless, the deceitful infection of the cultic promoters continues as they beguile unstable souls away from the clear and obvious truth of God into unprovable "mysteries" that they themselves cannot explain. They talk in long discourses, asking many questions, but giving no real answers. Their speech is mere circumlocution.

One of God's gifts to His true ministers is the ability to take the mysteries of God and make them plain. **Seeing then that we have such hope, we use great plainness of speech" (2 Corinthians 3:12).** The normal direction of the cultic promoter and false prophet is to take the plain truth of the Word of God and turn it into a mysterious message. The word "occult" means secret or hidden, thus we can see this is one method Satan uses to deceive those who do not know the Word of God. Clarity of belief is one of the characteristics of true Christianity.

Cults and the occult discourage the operation of the whole

40

man. They stress either the spiritual part of man, the soulish part of man (mind, emotions and will), or the physical man. Many are encouraged to become so spiritual as to ignore all the other needs of life. They are not to think or reason but to accept spiritual truths only as taught by those in authority. The mind is unimportant according to them. This is completely contrary to Scripture for the Word of God tells us to channel our thoughts into certain areas and not others. We are told in **Phillipians 4:7-8: And the peace of God, which passeth all understanding, shall keep your hearts and minds through Christ Jesus. Finally, brethren, whatsoever things are true, whatsoever things are honest, whatsoever things are just, whatsoever things are pure, whatsoever things are lovely, whatsoever things are of good report; if there be any virtue, and if there be any praise, think on these things.**

False Meditation

Meditation groups encourage people to blank out their minds which leaves them open for demonic influences. As Christians, we are instructed to think soberly, not to leave our minds blank. We are to love God with all of our mind and soul, as well as our spirit. **Jesus said unto him, Thou shalt love the Lord thy God with all thy heart, and with all thy soul, and with all thy mind. This is the first and great commandment (Matthew 22:37-38).**

Many cults prey on people with passive natures so they can implant their ideas and thoughts without any resistance from them. Some groups emphasize physical pleasure, while others stress extreme physical denial. The trinity of man is either ignored or pushed out of balance, thus allowing the enemy to take his toll in the lives of many victims.

Many false doctrines overstress the separation of the spirit and body of man by allowing the body to sin, claiming that the spirit is holy and does not sin no matter what the body or soul does. In *Healing of Spirit, Soul and Body*, we do a complete study on this showing that the spirit, soul and body are a functioning unit, and the proper order for their function is the reborn spirit in charge of the soul (mind, emotions and will) with the body in subjection to them.

False religions also go to extremes by teaching asceticism which abuses the body of man. All natural physical desires and pleasures are thought to be evil, so rigorous self-denial is practiced for religious purposes. Some teach that even sex in marriage is unholy, thus eventually destroying those marriages.

Legalism Without Mercy

Another earmark of cults and the occult is the extreme legalism which exists within their organizations. In their legalistic approach to the Scriptures, they set up rules and regulations that must be kept while mercy and faith are omitted. Jesus spoke about the scribes and Pharisees of His day being guilty of the same thing.

Woe unto you, scribes and Pharisees, hypocrites! for ye pay tithe of mint and anise and cummin, and have omitted the weightier matters of the law, judgment, mercy, and faith: these ought ye to have done, and not to leave the other undone (Matthew 23:23).

The leaders of these cults elevate themselves as exalted messiahs and are presumptuous egotists. If we are aware of these organized heresies, we can keep ourselves and others from becoming involved.

Review of False Doctrines

In review, the cults and occult are devoted to a religious view or leader that is centered in false doctrine. Identifying marks are extra-Biblical revelation; salvation outside of Jesus Christ; manipulation of followers through fear; bondage to organizational rules; egocentric leadership; financial exploitation; secrecy; basic Bible doctrines perverted; partial Bible truths taught in extremes, and/or the claim that only their group is going to heaven.

Cultic Involvement Brings a Curse

The danger of becoming involved with these groups is very grave as the Lord has pronounced a curse on all Satanic involvement. Many suffer today from demonic harassment that takes such forms as abnormal fears, nightmares, unusual and tormenting sights and sounds, freak accidents, fatal illnesses, and torturous diseases which are directly attributable to cultic involvement.

Many Christians are not even aware that their involvement in any of these organizations (past or present) opens the door for demonic influences and attacks. Looking to God's Word, He clearly warns and admonishes us to avoid these cults and cultic practices.

When thou art come into the land which the Lord thy God giveth thee, thou shalt not learn to do after the abominations of those nations. There shall not be found among you any one that maketh his son or his daughter to pass through the fire, or that useth divination, or an observer of times, or an enchanter, or a witch, or a charmer, or a consulter with familiar spirits, or a wizard, or a necromancer. For all that do these things are an abomination unto the Lord: and because of these abominations the Lord thy God doth drive them out from before thee. Thou shalt be perfect with the Lord thy God. For these nations, which thou shalt possess, hearkened unto observers of times, and unto diviners: but as for thee, the Lord thy God hath not suffered thee so to do (Deuteronomy 18:9-14).

Many people are ignorantly engaged in things that are an abomination unto the Lord because they are not aware of the

Scriptures that give such solemn warnings to stay away from these things.

Satanic Witchcraft Power

Deuteronomy 18:10 begins with a list of things that are condemned by God. **There shall not be found among you any one that maketh his son or his daughter to pass through the fire.** An evil spirit is behind this and the Thai Buddhists still practice firewalking today. Through Satan's power they are kept from being physically burned, but their souls are brought into spiritual bondage ultimately leading to an eternal hell-fire.

"Divination" follows, and here again we find people engaging in this by seeking counsel from fortune tellers, palm readers, spiritualists, etc. Satan gives these people certain knowledge through a divining spirit, but the bare thread of truth also ends up wrapping its victims' souls in cords of wickedness.

One of the most prevalent forms of witchcraft, in which many Christians are blindly trapped, is that of "observing times." The common names for this are astrology, horoscope, and almanac consulting. In recent years this practice has become quite common and the question, "What sign are you born under?" is heard everywhere. This abomination is subtle because many think it is harmless and fun even though they say they do not believe in it themselves. We can never tamper with the works of darkness even "in fun" and expect to come out untouched. Many people are suffering depression just from partaking in this sin. It also can produce a spirit of division that splits homes and causes rebellion in children. Many people do not acknowledge that their problems are spiritual, but instead blame their mates, children, jobs, circumstances or a host of other things for the trouble existing in their lives. All the while involvement with these evils mentioned continues to produce their distress.

Other forms of witchcraft are Satan worshipers, those involved in black masses, white and black witches, charmers (ranging from the snake charmers to those that cast spells and supposedly ward off evil), consulters with familiar spirits, wizards (those practicing sorcery, the Greek word for sorcery is "pharmakia" from which our modern day word for pharmacy is derived; drugs, spells, potions, and poisons are used by wizards), necromancers (mediums who practice seances for the purpose of conjuring up the dead -- these are really evil spirits impersonating the dead).

There is a curse on all who are in any way involved in these sins and abominations.

Therefore shall evil come upon thee; thou shalt not know from whence it riseth: and mischief shall fall upon thee; thou shalt not be able to put it off: and desolation shall come upon thee suddenly, which thou shalt not know. Stand now with thine enchantments, and with the multitude of thy sorceries, wherein thou hast laboured from thy youth; if so be thou shalt be able to profit, if so be thou mayest prevail. Thou art wearied in the multitude of thy counsels. Let now the astrologers, the stargazers, the monthly prognosticators, stand up, and save thee from these things that shall come upon thee. Behold, they shall be as stubble; the fire shall burn them; they shall not deliver themselves from the power of the flame: there shall not be a coal to warm at, nor fire to sit before it (Isaiah 47:11-14).

How can we escape the curse and be set free from the consequences that come from being involved with any of these things? First, we must be honest with God and admit our sin (even if we were ignorant at the time); next, we must repent and renounce all ties with the past in those areas which the Lord says are an abomination to Him.

Satanic Objects Must Be Destroyed

Some of these ties could be objects that were used in cult

and occult practices. These objects represent Satan and therefore we need to cleanse our home of them. We are commanded to do so in Scripture. **Deuteronomy 7:25-26** states, **The graven images of their gods shall ye burn with fire: thou shalt not desire the silver or gold that is on them, nor take it unto thee, lest thou be snared therein: for it is an abomination to the Lord thy God. Neither shalt thou bring an abomination into thine house, lest thou be a cursed thing like it: but thou shalt utterly detest it, and thou shalt utterly abhor it; for it is a cursed thing.**

Many Christians have brought idols and other works of evil into their homes without realizing the harm and curse that also comes in with them. Idols or statues that others use for worship are specifically forbidden in Scripture. Statues of Buddha are one of the most common idols seen in homes. Satan has deceived people by presenting these as decorator items. Objects such as these should be burned or destroyed, for they open lives up to Satanic bondage and attack.

Antichrist Symbols

Some objects or idols are not recognized as such because of the traditions of men. We need to ask the Holy Spirit to give us wisdom and discernment regarding these. These items are worn as jewelry and seem innocent until the Holy Spirit reveals them for what they are.

For example, there is a piece of jewelry worn by Christians that is really an old Egyptian fertility symbol. This is called the "ankh." It looks like a cross except for the oval circle at its top.

Mood rings are in the same category; also, jewelry and emblems bearing the "peace sign" as this is referred to in witchcraft as the "broken cross," mocking Jesus' death.

The "Star of David" is another popular jewelry piece worn by Christians who ignorantly honor their presumed Jewish heritage. God does love the Jewish people as all other people; however, He is displeased with the Jewish religion, Judaism, as it has eliminated Jesus as the Messiah. Therefore it is a false religion. **I know that ye are Abraham's seed; but ye seek to kill me, because my word hath no place in you (John 8:37).** Jews that continue in error are lost and not "chosen," but rather disinherited.

Neither, because they are the seed of Abraham, are they all children: but, In Isaac shall thy seed be called. That is, They which are the children of the flesh, these are not the children of God: but the children of the promise are counted for the seed (Romans 9:7-8).

And if ye be Christ's, then are ye Abraham's seed, and heirs according to the promise (Galatians 3:29) & (John 14:7)

In my opinion we should not wear items that represent Jewish doctrine as it is a false religion. The "Star of David" is actually the same six pointed star forming the "hexagram" that witches use in black masses when casting spells or placing "hexes" on people. The Greek word for six is "hex." The number six in the Bible represents evil or man's number as we note the number of the beast in **Revelation 13:18** is "666." The "Star of David" is never mentioned in the Bible and is not of Christian origin. It is of witchcraft origination and is used by several cults in their rites. We find it also listed in the Masonic encyclopedia along with several other antichristian symbols.

Many times those who wear antichristian symbols invite the works of darkness in, such as depression, lust, moodiness, sickness, accidents, fear, etc. We should also check our homes to see what kind of pictures we have on the walls, and check our closets for old souvenirs of the past and ask the Holy Spirit to show us the things of darkness that should not be in our homes. It would be wise to throw out the old weather witches (don't become involved with "water witching" either), ouija boards, wooden spoons with evil faces from foreign islands, excessive owl and frog decorator items, Sun gods, Confucius paintings, images of serpents

47

and dragons, voodoo dolls, Kachina dolls, Yeibichai designs on Indian rugs, Indian "god's eyes" made with yarn, etc. **(2 Kings 23:7).**

Several items that people use especially in the Southwestern part of the U.S.A. have their origin in American Indian witchcraft. If we have these things in our home, office, or possession, we will find a world of darkness upon our lives. The encyclopedia clearly defines these things as emblems of the Indian gods. Some of the protection or blessing emblems used by them are:

God's eye -- wall decoration made of yarn -- medicine man's watchful eye

Thunderbird -- jewelry, pottery, etc. -- sacred bearer of unlimited happiness

Arrow -- protection by the gods

Totem Poles -- faces of gods; Indian tribes offer prayer to them

Squash blossom -- Used on jewelry; the pendant is shaped to look like the moon in its first or last quarter; it is a fertility symbol.

Snake -- sign meaning defiance and wisdom

Bear track -- supposedly a good omen

Cedar wood masks -- owl spirit which is their guardian of the night

All of these items should be burned and discarded (not given away or sold as they would then bring harm to others). This might seem extreme to some but **Deuteronomy 7:25** says, **...thou shalt not desire the silver or gold that is on them.** Do we want to obey the Lord more than we desire the money these things represent?

If these things belong to members of our family that do not yet understand the evil involved, we should bind the power of Satan that would come through the object and ask God to bring that family member into the knowledge of the light. However, if children are involved we must use the authority God has given us as parents and refuse to allow them to bring evil into the house regardless of whether they understand or not. Of course, we should pray before attempting to rid their rooms of evil things, and if the children are old enough, we should speak to them about what we are doing. However, if they are not willing to part with these things, we must go ahead and see to it that the items are removed.

Must Rid Your Home of Witchcraft

Rock music tapes and albums are one of the greatest evils in people's lives. Even some so-called "Jesus rock" is destructive, as the beat in these albums has its origin in witchcraft. Testing music as to its origin is done by examining what it produces. Does it excite the flesh or does it inspire worship in our hearts toward God? Posters with rock singers, or faces of evil, or movie stars that are known for their open sin should all be discarded. Science fiction movies and movies showing witchcraft practices and television programs promoting worldly and evil influences should also be avoided. Books and shirts advertising these things should be destroyed also. Many parents do not understand why rebellion is so strong in their children, not seeing that involvement in these things is the very culprit that is producing it as these are forms of witchcraft.

These evils were designed by the devil and are forms of witchcraft which lead to terrible sins of lust, sex sin and drug involvement. It is not easy to get a child free of these chains after long periods of involvement. It takes much prayer, love and all-out warfare against Satan. He does not like to turn loose of those in his traps. Children involved in these evils must have the prayer of deliverance prayed over them, for there is a demon that must be dealt with in these cases. The power of the Holy Spirit is the only thing that can permanently free someone from rock music and drugs.

Other things that are abominations to God are books or games on witchcraft, horror, the occult, wizards, horoscopes, astrology, mind control, transcendental meditation, reincarnation, Jean Dixon

49

prophecies, Edgar Cayce books and other similar writings. God says very clearly in **Ephesians 4:27, Neither give place to the devil.** We must rid our lives of all that offends God. In **Acts 19:18-19**, we find the early Christians had to do the same thing. **And many that believed came, and confessed, and shewed their deeds. Many of them also which used curious arts brought their books together, and burned them before all men: and they counted the price of them, and found it fifty thousand pieces of silver.**

There is, however, an extreme to be avoided in dealing with objects. Some people begin seeing demons in everything. Satan can push us to an extreme of unnessarily destroying certain items. If we have a question about an article, we simply need to ask the Holy Spirit if it needs destroying. If objects that are not of an occult nature are in question (perhaps because of their ownership by someone evil), the Lord will give us His wisdom in the matter if we seek Him. Where neutral objects are in question we can simply exercise our spiritual authority and command all evil ties to be broken over them.

Binding Powers of Darkness

We have been given power over objects; the objects do not hold power over us. Many Christians are inadvertently exposed to evil objects in their places of employment, stores, friend's homes, etc. However, these have no power against the Christian who exercises his faith over them. We are in the world but not of the world. **I pray not that thou shouldest take them out of the world, but that thou shouldest keep them from the evil. They are not of the world, even as I am not of the world. Sanctify them through thy truth: thy word is truth (John 17:15-17).**

As we pray for those who are deceived and do not know the truth of God's Word regarding evil objects, we will see the Lord begin moving in the lives of those people. Until they see the light, we can simply bind the powers of darkness in the objects around them. This will help release them and bring them into the truth.

Watch Your Words

There are words and expressions that should be avoided in the Christian vocabulary such as "luck" or "lucky," also the so-called "good luck" charms such as rabbit's feet. The definition of luck is "something that happens to one by chance." This then leaves us open for "good luck" and "bad luck." As Christians, we do not live by chance or fate, but by faith in the Son of the living God. Our lives are destined that we might become overcomers in Him.

Other words that are unhealthy and negative are expressions such as, "She makes me sick," "I am dying to go," "It frightened me to death," and "I doubt if he will ever change." All these words express negative confessions and should be avoided as sickness, death, fear and doubt come from the devil. We need to ask the Lord to clean up our vocabulary.

Swearing and cursing are not the only sins of the mouth that need to be dealt with and put away. We must be serious about living in the light of God's Word. We are told in **Ephesians 5:4-12, Neither filthiness, nor foolish talking, nor jesting, which are not convenient: but rather giving thanks. For this ye know, that no whoremonger, nor unclean person, nor coveteous man, who is an idolater, hath any inheritance in the kingdom of Christ and of God. Let no man deceive you with vain words: for because of these things cometh the wrath of God upon the children of disobedience. Be not ye therefore partakers with them. For ye were sometimes darkness, but now are ye light in the Lord: walk as children of light: (For the fruit of the Spirit is in all goodness and righteousness and truth;) Proving what is acceptable unto the Lord. And have no fellowship with the unfruitful works of darkness, but rather reprove them.**

After admitting our sin, repenting and asking for a cleansing of our spiritual and physical houses, the next step is to take authority over the powers of darkness that have kept us deceived and held in these traps of the enemy. Believers in Christ Jesus have the power to do this because evil spirits must flee if they are commanded to do so in the name of Jesus. **And these signs shall follow them that believe; In my name shall they cast out devils... (Mark 16:17).**

3

The World of Demons

Willful Sin Brings Demonic Attacks

The majority of Christians today are totally ignorant of the nature of evil spirits (demons), and many would prefer that they were not even mentioned. They choose to ignore this portion of God's ministry because they are fearful of things beyond their understanding. The result of this ignorance is that multitudes live in needless torment. One of the deadliest misrepresentations of the truth of God is that a Christian should not be concerned with thoughts that a demon could be their problem. This is taught within many churches and gives the devil a "field day" to bring fear, mental torment, jealousy, hatred, lust, pride, self-pity, addiction, gluttony and many other forms of bondage, oppression, and defilement.

When we practice willful sin, Satan eventually sends one of his demons that is compatible with that particular sin to dwell within us. Then each time we give way to that sin that spirit takes over. Since their personalities mesh with those of their victims, it takes spiritual discernment to detect them. We must remember that demon spirits are "invisible beings" with wicked intelligence that seek bodies in which they can express themselves. These spirits are emissaries sent from Satan having personalities and characteristics that make up an intelligent being. They walk, hear, speak, see, obey, seek, think, know and dwell in the body to accomplish their evil purposes (**Matthew 12:43-45, Mark 1:23-24,3:11**). They are made subject to Christ and believers by the atonement, the name of Jesus, and the Holy Spirit. Each principal demon or "strongman" has a particular mission which we are able to recognize by its fruit or manifestation. We need to seek God and study His Word to find the truth about this controversial subject.

Can a Christian Have a Demon?

One of Satan's clever devices is to cause division among Christians over just such a subject, for then he is allowed to work freely on both sides. One side refuses to believe that a Christian can have a demon, while the other side sees demons in everything. Both sides are extreme, but if we look to God's Word we can find balance. To answer the question, "Can a Christian have a demon?" we need to understand the two main causes of a Christian's problems.

The first problem is what Paul calls the "flesh" in **Romans 8:5-8, For they that are after the flesh do mind the things of the flesh; but they that are after the Spirit the things of the Spirit. For to be carnally minded is death; but to be spiritually minded is life and peace. Because the carnal mind is enmity against God: for it is not subject to the law of God, neither indeed can be. So then they that are in the flesh cannot please God.** Yielding to the "flesh" is sin.

The "flesh" is defined here as the "carnal mind" and it is spoken of as enmity with God. The carnal mind is in the soul of man. After a Christian experiences the "new birth," he is a new creature; however, he finds he still has the problem of walking in the flesh instead of the Spirit. His mind has not been renewed yet by the Word of God, so unless he reckons the "old man" dead when tempted, he fails God and gives in to his "flesh." To maintain a walk in the Spirit one must totally dedicate his life to God and continually choose the path of God.

The "flesh" of man is under Satan's dominion as it is part of the old Adamic nature. The "flesh" and the "world" are under Satan's influence, so when we sin we have yielded to an attack by Satan in an indirect way. **Romans 6:16, Know ye not, that to whom ye yield yourselves, servants to obey, his servants ye are to whom ye obey; whether of sin unto death, or of obedience unto righteousness.**

The way to get rid of the devil in these instances is to submit to the Lord and resist Satan so that he will flee (**James 4:7**). We are to crucify the flesh and choose God's way in the situation. **And they that are Christ's have crucified the flesh with the affections and lusts (Galatians 5:24).**

Filthiness in Flesh and Spirit

The second cause of a Christian's inner problems is evil spirits or demons which Satan uses to fasten upon some aspect of the "flesh" that has not yet been overcome. These demons do not relinquish their hold unless compelled to do so. Some argue that a Christian cannot have a demon in him. They say he now has Christ in his spirit, and the Spirit of Christ and evil spirits cannot co-exist. Because of this erroneous teaching, many are bound by dark powers when they could be free. This is contrary to Scripture as also James is speaking to Christians when he admonishes them in **James 4:5, Do ye think that the scripture saith in vain, the spirit that dwelleth in as lusteth to envy? II Corinthians 7:1** states, **Having therefore these promises, dearly beloved, let us cleanse ourselves from all filthiness of the flesh and spirit, perfecting holiness in the fear of God.**

The Holy Spirit certainly needs no cleansing, but man's soul or flesh has filth in it and many times filthy (unclean) spirits need to be cast out. Jesus talked about our bodies being houses. He made it plain that if, after cleaning, we were not continually filled with the Holy Spirit, a demon could return.

When the unclean spirit is gone out of a man, he walketh through dry places, seeking rest, and findeth none. Then he saith, I will return into my house from whence I came out; and when he is come, he findeth it empty, swept, and garnished. Then goeth he, and taketh with himself seven other spirits more wicked than himself, and they enter in and dwell there: and the last state of that man is worse than the first.

Even so shall it be also unto this wicked generation (Matthew 12:43-45).

By this Scripture it may be seen that a portion of the kingdom of Satan is a host of bodiless spirits. They seek to enter the bodies of mortals or beasts, and their work is greatly enhanced when hidden in the bodies of men. **And all the devils besought him, saying Send us into the swine, that we may enter into them (Mark 5:12).** Demons perform their evil deeds and their victims are blamed for them. Certainly people are responsible for the sin which allowed this demonic activity within, but they are driven past what they intended, as the evil personality takes over their actions.

Chains of Iniquity

Some children are born under a curse and have demons that cause their erratic behavior. Parents are in ignorance as to why some children beat their heads on the floor in rages, scream and yell uncontrollably, bite themselves, or have continual nightmares. Many children do have demons and need to be set free. There is an account of this in **Mark 9:20-21, And they brought him unto him: and when he saw him, straightway the spirit tare him; and he fell on the ground, and wallowed foaming. And he asked his father, How long is it ago since this came unto him? And he said, Of a child.**

Demons can attack with no sin involved on the victims' part as in the case of children. The sins of the fathers bring a curse, and there is a "chain of iniquity" that needs to be broken. **Thou shalt not bow down thyself to them, nor serve them: for I the Lord thy God am a jealous God, visiting the iniquity of the fathers upon the children unto the third and fourth generation of them that hate me; And shewing mercy unto thousands of them that love me, and keep my commandments (Exodus 20:5-6).** Additional Scripture talking about the "chains of iniquity" is found in **Jeremiah 32:18, Thou showest loving-kindness unto thousands, and recompensest the inquity of the fathers into the bosom of their children after them; the Great, the Mighty God, the Lord of hosts, is his name.** Also **Jeremiah 16:19** and **Isaiah. 14:20-22** show how we can inherit spiritual curses because of our father's or ancestor's evil deeds.

Demons can also enter when the person's will is weakened and he is overpowered by the devil. This happens many times when a person goes through a terrible shock or experiences an incident that produces extreme fear. Accident victims who are knocked unconscious due to blows on the head often are subject to demon invasion. Addicts and alcoholics eventually have demons as the drugs and alcohol suppress their wills leaving them open for attack.

Demons are invited in by persons who yield to sin continually. The demon personality is compatible with the particular sin the person is entertaining. If the Lord is not sought to set the person free, one demon will invite others and the person will be possessed, even as Mary Magdalene was with seven demons. **And certain women, which had been healed of evil spirits and infirmities, Mary called Magdalene, out of whom went seven devils (Luke 8:2).**

Many people desire to be free, yet continue to find themselves in bondage. Recognizing the need for deliverance is the first step to freedom. Before coming to Christ, man takes all kinds of things into his heart and spirit and one of the first works of the Holy Spirit is to begin cleaning his "spiritual house."

A beautiful "type" of this is the incident of Jesus cleansing the temple that had been defiled by those who were wicked.

And Jesus went into the temple of God, and cast out all them that sold and bought in the temple, and overthrew the tables of the moneychangers, and the seats of them that sold doves, And said unto them, It is written, My house shall be called the house of prayer; but ye have made it a den of thieves (Matthew 21:12-13).

We are now the temple of God and when the Holy Spirit comes into our lives, He begins the same process of "casting out" those things that offend Him. **And what agreement hath the temple of God with idols? for ye are the temple of the living God; as God hath said, I will dwell in them, and walk in them; and I will be their God, and they shall be my people (2 Corinthians 6:16).**

Demons Enslave People to a Sin

This cleansing process sometimes happens automatically at the time of salvation simply due to God's grace and our ignorance of demons even existing. However, some do not continue to walk in the freedom of God's Spirit and therefore fall back into the world. All their old habits return to haunt them. They then try to get the victory, but find something is controlling them that is stronger than their wills. They have given place to the devil. **Ephesians 4:22-32** warns us not to give in to the old man thus giving place to the devil.

There are three main identifying marks of evil spirits. They enslave, they defile and they torment. If a person has renounced evil and committed his life to Christ but still has not found peace, the problem is very likely due to the influence of evil spirits. The sooner one recognizes this evil force and accepts God's way of being freed, the sooner he can go on to a normal, happy life.

The need for deliverance in Christians is common and should not be viewed as freakish or out of the ordinary. Throughout Jesus' earthly ministry, great emphasis was placed upon casting out demons. He not only personally freed people from demons, but He commissioned His followers to do likewise and gave them the authority to use His name to achieve this miracle.

And they were astonished at his doctrine: for he taught them as one that had authority, and not as the scribes. And there was in their synagogue a man with an unclean spirit;

and he cried out, Saying, Let us alone; what have we to do with thee, thou Jesus of Nazareth? art thou come to destroy us? I know thee who thou art, the Holy One of God. And Jesus rebuked him, saying, Hold thy peace, and come out of him. And when the unclean spirit had torn him, and cried out with a loud voice, he came out of him. And they were all amazed, insomuch that they questioned among themselves, saying, What thing is this? what new doctrine is this? for with authority commandeth he even the unclean spirits, and they do obey him (Mark 1:22-27).

After these things the Lord appointed other seventy also, and sent them two and two before his face into every city and place, whither he himself would come.....And the seventy returned again with great joy, saying, Lord, even the devils are subject unto us through thy name (Luke 10:1, 17).

The problem of demons was a common one and Jesus dealt with it continually in His ministry. **And he healed many that were sick of divers diseases, and cast out many devils; and suffered not the devils to speak, because they knew him (Mark 1:34).**

We find accounts of this same ministry in the lives of Peter, Paul and Philip.

And the people with one accord gave heed unto those things which Philip spake, hearing and seeing the miracles which he did. For unclean spirits, crying with loud voice, came out of many that were possessed with them; and many taken with palsies, and that were lame, were healed. And there was great joy in that city (Acts 8:6-8).

There came also a multitude out of the cities round about unto Jerusalem, bringing sick folks, and them which were vexed with unclean spirits: and they were healed every one (Acts 5:16).

These people that were coming to Philip for deliverance were spoken of as "giving heed to the things he spoke." We know Philip was an evangelist so he was speaking the salvation message and many of these people had to be saved if they were obeying what he preached. Therefore, they were Christians who needed deliverance.

Demons Can Cause Sickness

The solution to any demon problem is to have it "cast out." The gift of discerning of spirits **(2 Corinthians 12:10)** is provided by the Lord to aid in setting people free from evil spirits. God has set members in the body of Christ who have been given this gift.

Sometimes an evil spirit is not the problem and the person may need healing instead. In other cases this works vice versa where people have been prayed over and over for healing to no avail because they need a demon cast out which is causing the sickness. We find an account of this in **Luke 13:11-13, And, behold, there was a woman which had a spirit of infirmity eighteen years, and was bowed together, and could in no wise lift up herself. And when Jesus saw her, he called her to him, and said unto her, Woman, thou art loosed from thine infirmity. And he laid his hands on her: and immediately she was made straight, and glorified God.**

This woman responded when the spirit of infirmity left her. In **Luke 13:16** Jesus also states, in reply to the ruler of the synagogue's criticism of healing on the sabbath, **And ought not this woman, being a daughter of Abraham, whom Satan hath bound, lo, these eighteen years, be loosed from this bond on the sabbath day?** Here we can see that Satan had her bound and that the sickness was from him. Jesus came to set the captives free, and many were delivered from satanic powers of darkness.

Jesus said in **Luke 4:18, The Spirit of the Lord is upon me, because he hath anointed me to preach the gospel to the poor; he hath sent me to heal the brokenhearted, to preach deliverance to the captives, and recovering of sight to the blind,**

**to set at liberty them that are bruised, To preach the accept-
able year of the Lord**.

Today, the Lord is still sending forth the gospel to the poor
as missionaries are being sent to virtually every country. He does
not want to stop with just "half" the gospel preached but desires
that the concurrent messages of salvation, deliverance and healing be preached and administered. The full gospel message is
needed desperately today, just as it was needed then. Human hearts
have not changed, demons have not changed and God has not
changed. God is healing and delivering all today who come to
Him in faith, just as He did then. The only difference is that Jesus
was limited to a physical body then, but now He comes in the
person of the Holy Spirit and all who have the Holy Spirit have
access to His power. Praise God!

Possession

Satan's plan is to weaken people to a point where they sin,
giving him a legal right then to enter. One can sin for awhile without coming under bondage. However, if one continues to submit
to him, the devil soon will take hold of ground in that area of their
lives. They become possessed or "held" in that particular area.
We need to define posses-sion as it causes much confusion when
used without understanding its Greek meaning.

Possession means "to hold"; therefore, when anyone is out
of control in an area, Satan is said to have a "stronghold" there.
The person has lost control and Satan has gained it, thereby holding him captive. He is not totally possessed as this would mean
the devil had control of spirit, soul and body. Total possession
requires the surrender of one's will. Satan's plan is to bring people
to this place by progressively taking more and more territory in
their lives. Only the power of Christ can set people free from
demons.

We have all heard the old saying about the man who takes a

drink, then the drink takes a drink and finally the drink takes the man. Possession is progressive. If we allow Satan into one area of our lives, soon he takes more territory. **Ephesians 4:27** admonishes us, **Neither give place to the devil.**

Oppression or Possession?

Some people teach that a Christian can only by "oppressed" of the devil, but not "possessed." When we have a problem with the devil, we find that it is difficult battling him, no matter if he is on the outside shoving us around or if he is on the inside leading us about. The real message we need to get into our spirits is that we need to know how to overcome the devil whether he is on the outside or the inside. The devil gets mileage from the argument of whether a Christian can have a demon or not, defeating the debaters at every turn.

James 3:10 states a problem that many Christians have before they are delivered. **Out of the same mouth proceedeth blessing and cursing. My brethren, these things ought not so to be.** James is talking to Christians here for he calls them his brethren. **James 3:6** says the tongue is the instrument the devil uses to ensnare us. **And the tongue is a fire, a world of iniquity: so is the tongue among our members, that it defileth the whole body, and setteth on fire the course of nature; and it is set on fire of hell.** The whole body can be defiled by the tongue.

Sinning Can Lead to Possession

Possession does not necessarily mean one is filled with demons and completely out of control. Possession is by degree. By continuing to sin, Satan gets a stronger "hold." The reason "possession" has such a derogatory meaning to us is because we generally relate it to the possession story in the Bible of the Gadarene demoniac found in **Luke 8:26-36**. Since he had more than 5,000 demons (a legion is 5,000), he was virtually totally possessed. The Lord Jesus looked on his heart and knew the man wanted to be free, so He commanded the devils to leave him. The story reads as follows:

And they arrived at the country of the Gadarenes, which is over against Galilee. And when he went forth to land, there met him out of the city a certain man, which had devils long time, and ware no clothes, neither abode in any house, but in the tombs. When he saw Jesus, he cried out, and fell down before him, and with a loud voice said, What have I to do with thee, Jesus, thou Son of God most high? I beseech thee, torment me not. (For he had commanded the unclean spirit to come out of the man. For oftentimes it had caught him: and he was kept bound with chains and in fetters; and he brake the bands, and was driven of the devil into the wilderness.) And Jesus asked him, saying, What is thy name? And he said, Legion: because many devils were entered into him. And they besought him that he would not command them to go out into the deep. And there was there an herd of many swine feeding on the mountain: and they besought him that he would suffer them to enter into them. And he suffered them. Then went the devils out of the man, and entered into the swine: and the herd ran violently down a steep place into the lake, and were choked. When they that fed them saw what was done, they fled, and went and told it in the city and in the country. Then they went out to see what was done; and came to Jesus, and found the man, out of whom the devils were departed, sitting at the feet of Jesus, clothed, and in his right mind: and they were afraid. They also which saw it told them by what means he that was possessed of the devils was healed.

Mental Illness Linked to Demons

We can learn several things about devils from this account. We see that mental illness can be attributed to demons. Insanity is a major problem in the world today, and not many people realize that deliverance could set free many beset with it. Psychiatrists offer no permanent cures for these disturbed people, as most of them do not know they are dealing with a spiritual problem. The Gadarene demoniac returned to his right mind when the devils left.

Why did Jesus allow the demons to enter the herd of swine instead of sending them back to the deep (hell)? It would appear that the Lord wanted to demonstrate an object lesson here. People of that day probably had as much trouble accepting the reality of evil spirits as people today do. Jesus allowed those evil spirits to enter the swine so that the people would understand this man's problem was demon possession. If they simply left, the people would think he received a healing instead of a deliverance. When the evil spirits entered the swine, the destructive nature of the demons created violence and caused the immediate death of the herd.

Demons Destroy Through Suicide and Divorce

Many people today are being driven to suicide because of demon possession. They need help and deliverance. People do not want to face the fact that their problem could be demonic, and so Satan robs another life with his evil spirits. It does not matter how many demons someone has, one is enough to destroy him. We need to separate the demon personality from the person. Marriages split up today because unclean spirits lie to one or both mates and lead them to walk away from families even after years of wedlock. Women say they do not understand why their husbands suddenly walked away without any previous major problems. They claim their mates acted strangely and then suddenly divorced them without any real cause. Women have deserted not only their husbands, but their children as well, and have simply disappeared or left with another man.

What evil force is behind these splits? Satan has sent his evil spirits of division and has told his newest victim lies of a beautiful life with someone else. Of course, he supplies the necessary emotions for someone else and causes the deceived partner to no longer "feel" love for his or her mate. After he manages to separate a home, he then begins the process all over again with the next marriage. The innocent mates in these divided marriages many times comment, "I just don't understand, he (or she) simply did not act like himself; he was like a stranger when he asked for the divorce and told me he didn't love me any more." This "stranger" many times is a demon spirit that has the person deceived. Many marriages could be saved if Christians were taught how to battle in the Spirit and command the demons to depart from the deceived person. This can all be done through prayer.

Battling Against Demons

The Lord is revealing the devices of Satan so that Christians can learn to battle the real enemy as he attacks their marriages, instead of battling one another. The main thing we need to do is to take authority over Satan, casting him out of our lives and the lives of our loved ones. Satan is a robber and a thief, and he delights in destroying God's children. God wants us to grow up, stop acting like children by fighting with one another, and fight the real enemy, Satan. We need to lay down our lives for our mates and loved ones and be aggressive in prayer against the wiles of the enemy. He will flee when commanded to do so in the name of Jesus.

If the attack is from without, carried on by Satan's suggestions, temptations and influences, we still fight him the same way we would if he has gained access and entered the body with dominating control. We call on God with a humble heart and submit our entire lives to Him, and then aggressively resist the devil, commanding him to leave in the name of Jesus. We should speak this command out loud.

We need to realize also there are certain conditions one must meet in order to gain permanent deliverance from demon bondage. We first must be a child of God to receive help. If you are not "born again," simply invite Jesus to come into your heart and save your soul. Accept God's Word that says He loves you and wants to give you abundant life. **For God so loved the world, that He gave His only begotten Son, that whosoever believeth in Him should not perish, but have everlasting life (John 3:16). I am come that they might have life, and that they might have it more abundantly (John 10:10).**

To receive this abundant life you must repent and turn from your sins and accept God's provision of the shed blood of Jesus Christ as the only way to cleanse you. Sin has separated you from God, and receiving Christ restores you to fellowship with Him and you become a part of the family of God. **But as many as received Him, to them gave he power to become the sons of God... (John 1:12).**

Prayers of Deliverance

After making a verbal confession of our faith in Jesus Christ (the only name that brings deliverance), we need to confess the sin that gave the devil access to our life. This is where we need to acknowledge any cult or occult involvement. Next, we should break Satan's legal right to our lives by renouncing each sin and its effect upon our lives as a lie of the devil, and then claim the truth of God's Word in that area. To be free from deception we must recognize Satan's lies and replace them with the truth. After these steps, we then can out loud command the demons to go in the name of Jesus. When oppression or possession is severe it is helpful to have other believers pray with you.The prayer of deliverance should be made only by "born again," Spirit-filled believers. In **Acts 19:13-16**, the unbelieving seven sons of Sceva experimented with deliverance and met with disastrous results. "Born again" believers have nothing to fear. Jesus overcame Satan for us. Casting out demons lodged in others is not risky but requires faith. Should you lack the faith and boldness to cast out demons, ask the Lord to lead you to the person or persons who can pray the prayer of faith and set people free.

We need to discuss here some guidelines for "casting out demons." The lack of teaching in this area has led people to devise many means by which they attempt deliverance. These methods are varied and include wrestling and holding people down during deliverance, carrying on conversations with demons to discern the names of the spirits (which is futile as Satan is a liar and wouldn't tell the truth anyway. Discerning of spirits is the gift given to aid in deliverance). Also calling out endless lists of demons, and many other methods which we shall not name here. These methods will work if done in the name of Jesus, however when they are carried to extremes the enemy wastes a lot of time and energy.

These methods are usually not necessary, but God honors them many times because the practitioners are unsure of the proper procedures, and perhaps this is the only teaching to which they have been exposed. God sees their hearts and He knows they are trying to help people get free, so He delivers them in spite of the techniques.

Faith Delivers

The Biblical method for casting out demons would be to pray as the Holy Spirit directs. Usually this would be a prayer similar to this: "In the name of Jesus, I cast you unclean spirits out of this person." Should the Holy Spirit give you specific names of demons, these most generally would be for the benefit of the person who is receiving the deliverance as they may need to be aware of the nature of the demon that has held them in bondage, so as to resist him in the future. The most important thing is to listen to the Holy Spirit's direction regarding individual cases. Faith is the key to getting people free of demons. We must have faith when we pray that the demons will leave. If we believe they will leave instantly, then that will happen; if we believe we are in for a real battle, then we will end up fighting it out with the devil. Or we can even lose the battle if we don't stand firm in our faith and trust in Jesus. Some deliverance does require a prayer battle as no or little intercession as been previously done for the person bound.

Jesus' disciples had a problem with not being able to cast out a demon from a child because they lacked faith. When they asked Jesus why they couldn't do it, He answered in **Mark 9:19, 23, 26, 28, and 29: He answereth him, and saith, O faithless generation, how long shall I be with you? how long shall I suffer you? bring him unto me....Jesus said unto him, If thou canst believe, all things are possible to him that believeth....And the spirit cried, and rent him sore, and came out of him...And when he was come into the house, his disciples asked him privately, Why could not we cast him out? And he said unto them, This kind can come forth by nothing, but by prayer and fasting.**

The message Jesus was trying to get across to his disciples was that their faith was not sufficient for the job, and that the way their faith would be increased was by fasting and praying. He didn't mean for them to go fast and pray to get the demons out. Jesus was immediately able to cast him out because He was always praying, and He stayed close to the Father, thereby having faith and power over the devil at all times.

Jesus is our example. If we are not in close communion with the Father, how will we be able to hear His instructions when discerning and praying for deliverance. We need to fast and pray if we find our faith and closeness with God being attacked, then we will be able to exercise our faith when praying for others and see them set free in the name of Jesus.

Can Demons Be Transferred?

Some people are afraid to lay their hands on people when praying for evil spirits to come out as they are afraid they might enter into them. They should not even pray for deliverance of others if they are still battling fear, as the fear can allow the enemy to attack them. The placing of their hands on the person seeking deliverance is not the real problem, but rather it is the fear.

The Scripture used to support this teaching is the one referring to "Lay hands suddenly on no man..." If we look at this Scripture closely we find that it is often taken out of context, for this chapter refers to the laying on of hands when ordaining elders, not casting out demons. **Lay hands suddenly on no man, neither be partaker of other men's sins: keep thyself pure (1 Timothy 5:22).** Jesus touched lepers and all manner of sick and possessed people, and the sicknesses and demons always fled from Him. As believers, we have the same authority in the Spirit, and Satan must do as we command him. Some fear receiving demons from others who might "lay hands on them," so they do not allow anyone to touch them. Our faith can prevent this from happening as no one can transfer demons to us if we ask the Father to shield us from them. This can happen, however, if the person being prayed for is not aware of someone evil laying hands on him and praying for him. If the person being prayed for then opens his spirit to receive from the evil person, he could receive an evil spirit.

If we can receive the Holy Spirit by the laying on of hands, we can also receive evil spirits by the laying on of hands. However, if we only open our spirits to the Holy Spirit, we need never be afraid of anyone transmitting a demon to us. If we have fears or doubts about the people praying over us, we can pray silently this prayer to God even before others lay hands on us, "Father, I receive only your blessings from these people here today and I receive nothing that is not of you." Demons cannot be transferred unless an individual has an open door with sin in his life.

Pleading the Blood of Jesus

Pleading the blood of Jesus over people while praying for deliverance is another area that is misunderstood. Some people go to extremes pleading the blood over everyone and everything, as if it were a "fetish." Actually, this is another area where faith is involved. It is faith in what the blood of Jesus did for us, and not the words of pleading it. Our faith is in the shed blood of Jesus on Calvary that now frees us and cleanses us from all power of Satan and his demons. Fear is the most common device the devil uses to keep people from casting out demons. He tells people that have a desire to minister deliverance many lies in order to maintain his kingdom. He keeps them from exercising their spiritual authority by telling lies such as the following: "You can't cast out a demon because it will attack you and enter you; The devil is stronger than you and he will cause so many problems for you, you will wish you had never started casting demons out; You are too weak and the devil will overpower you," etc. These lies are only effective if we believe them. If we know the Word of God and our Lord Jesus, we know that Satan is the defeated one and that he must leave when told to do so. He is only a bluff.

Since demons are spirits, when we cast them out we do not destroy them; we only destroy their influence upon those they have attacked. We cannot kill a spirit. Spirits are eternal. The Bible does not specifically say where they go when they are cast out, but in the cases recorded they had to leave their present habitat, seek another, wander in dry places, or go back to the deep (hell). **When the unclean spirit is gone out of a man, he walketh** through dry places, seeking rest, and findeth none. Then he saith, I will return into my house from whence I came out; and when he is come, he findeth it empty, swept, and garnished. Then goeth he, and taketh with himself seven other spirits more wicked than himself, and they enter in and dwell there: and the last state of that man is worse than the first. Even so shall it be also unto this wicked generation. (Matthew 12:43-45).

And he besought him much that he would not send them away out of the country (Mark 5:10).

Most of the time deliverance is won by the prayers of others. But unless the person who seeks deliverance determines to stay free and be filled with the Holy Spirit, the enemy will return. Satan's power is not automatically cancelled out by the presence of Christ within us; we must do our part to maintain deliverance. One must continue to walk in faith and obedience to the Lord to prevent demons returning.

Manifestations of Demons

We must meet the conditions in the Word of God to remain filled with the Holy Spirit. Being filled with the Holy Spirit is not just a one-time happening. It is a daily filling. We must ask the Lord to fill us each day and maintain a right relationship with Him. We must read and apply God's Word daily to our lives. Our body is a temple and we must keep it filled, not just swept, else Satan's demons can come back. **John 5:14** says, **...Behold, thou art made whole: sin nor more, lest a worse thing come unto thee.** We must resist sin, follow the Lord, and grow strong by reading and using the Word of God against the devil. Satan can be overcome by the power of the Holy Spirit not only in our lives, but also in the lives of all who seek Him with their whole hearts.

We should also mention some of the manifestations that can occur when a person is receiving deliverance. Biblical accounts record demons causing their victims to cry, scream, weep, fall down as dead, wallow on the ground, foam at the mouth, etc. On occasion these things occur when casting out demons; however, these are the exceptions to the rule. Most of the time they merely leave, and the person simply feels a release or weight lifted from him. Deliverance can come with no physical outward sign of the spirit's departure. However, a spiritual breakthrough will always be evident. The person will know they have been freed when the Holy Spirit's power drives out the demons. Their changed life is evidence of that freedom. We should not allow demons to speak, but command them, as Jesus did, to be quiet. **And he healed many that were sick of divers diseases, and cast out many devils; and suffered not the devils to speak, because they knew him (Mark 1:34).** The Lord generally did not allow spirits to manifest, but if there was a need for the people to realize the reality of demons, He did so. The case of the Gaderene demoniac is an example of this (Mark 5). The same holds true today. When people doubt the relevance of the deliverance ministry, or the existence of demons, the Lord will allow demons to manifest physically just so those persons may realize the need for deliverance and seek the needed help to be free. The Lord is calling many of His people to this vital ministry because so many are crying for help in these last days.

Discerning Devils

You are probably dealing with an evil spirit or demon when you have a problem that is unreasonable, abnormal, tormenting, uncontrollable, enslaving, or addicting. The Bible speaks of several different kinds of evil spirits that can be behind overpowering sins. These are referred to in the New Testament as unclean (foul) spirits. There are 22 occasions cited in the Bible where unclean spirits were cast out by Jesus or by someone else using His name. These spirits attach themselves to unclean areas of our soulish nature, or the "flesh." Other evil spirits specifically named in the Bible are seducing spirits, a perverse spirit, a spirit of slumber, a sorrowful spirit, the spirit of jealousy, the spirit of antichrist, the spirit of whoredoms, the spirit of bondage, spirit of devils, the spirit of error, the spirit of divination, a dumb spirit, a familiar spirit and the spirit of fear.

Listed here are some of the areas within the soul that Satan attacks with his unclean spirits: fear, depression, anxiety, loneliness, self-pity, rejection, resentment, hate, rebellion, impatience, pride, unforgiveness, jealousy, envy, covetousness, lust, doubt, and greed.

Now the works of the flesh are manifest, which are these; Adultery, fornication, uncleanness, lasciviousness, Idolatry, witchcraft, hatred, variance, emulations, wrath, strife, seditions, heresies, Envyings, murders, drunkenness, revellings, and such like: of the which I tell you before, as I have also told you in time past, that they which do such things shall not inherit the kingdom of God. (Galatians 5:19-21).

Symptoms of Demonic Activity

Demonic activity in a person's life can manifest through the following symptoms: an uncontrollable temper, excesses of any kind, addictions to food, alcohol, tobacco, pills, drugs, rock music, obsessive urges, homosexuality, perverted sex acts, oral sex, masturbation, prostitution, evil imaginings, vile thoughts on sex, sadistic mental pictures, incest, child abuse, rape, murder, suicide, tormenting fears, terror, nightmares, insomnia, sleepwalking, talking in one's sleep, bed wetting, extreme shyness, grinding of teeth, unusual weakness, hyperactivity, intellectual memory amplified, loss of memory, insanity, low I.Q.s, extremely high I.Q.s, unrelieved grief, continual strife, materialism, impotency, frigidity, manias and phobias of every kind. Unclean spirits of infirmity attack the body and can manifest as tumors, cancers, crippling diseases, arthritis, blindness, ulcers, migraine headaches, hay fever, asthma, allergies, epilepsy, heart problems, fevers and many other torturous diseases. Records of such cases are spoken of in the New Testament. By casting out the demons the people were freed. **Matthew 17:14-15** and **18** records a case of a boy delivered from insanity.

And when they were come to the multitude, there came to him a certain man, kneeling down to him, and saying, Lord, have mercy on my son: for he is lunatick, and sore vexed: for ofttimes he falleth into the fire, and oft into the water....And Jesus rebuked the devil; and he departed out of him: and the child was cured from that very hour.

Mark 3:10-11 tells of others being set free. **For he healed many; insomuch that they pressed upon him for to touch him, as many as had plagues. And unclean spirits, when they saw him, fell down before him, and cried, saying, Thou art the Son of God.** Deaf and dumb mutes can be delivered as this is from an evil spirit also. **When Jesus saw that the people came running together, he rebuked the foul spirit, saying unto him, Thou dumb and deaf spirit, I charge thee, come out of him, and enter no more into him (Mark 9:25).** Another account of Jesus bringing healing by casting out devils is found in **Matthew 12:22-30**.

Seducing spirits are usually the spirits that influence those involved in false religions, cults and the occult. These deceiving and withcraft spirits manifest as religious spirits and can even counterfeit the true gifts of God. They also manifest in strange supernatural happenings, such as weird sights, sounds and smells. People have been visited by apparitions (ghosts), demons impersonating dead people or U.F.O. visitors when these demons are in operation. These visits usually happen as a direct result of involvement in cultic or occult practices. We are warned about these doctrines of devils. **Now the spirit speaketh expressly, that in the latter times some shall depart from the faith, giving heed to seducing spirits, and doctrines of devils (1 Timothy 4:1).** To be free from the curse that comes upon those involved in such things, one needs to seek God for deliverance.

Sins of our Fathers

Some people suffer under a curse that has come down upon them, not as a direct result of their own involvement in evil but because their parents or grandparents were partakers in such things. **Thou shalt have no other gods before me...Thou shalt not bow down thyself to them, nor serve them: for I the Lord thy God am a jealous God, visiting the iniquity of the fathers upon the children unto the third and fourth generation of them that hate me; And shewing mercy unto thousands of them that love me, and keep my commandments (Exodus 20:3 and 5-6).**

Thou shewest lovingkindness unto thousands, and recompensest the iniquity of the fathers into the bosom of their children after them: the Great, the Mighty God, The Lord of hosts, is his name, Great in counsel, and mighty in work: for thine eyes are open upon all the ways of the sons of men: to give every one according to his ways, and according to the fruit of his doings (Jeremiah 32:18-19).

From these verses we see that a "chain of iniquity" comes down upon us from our forefathers who have sinned. On the positive side, we receive unmerited blessings if our fathers obeyed and walked in the Lord's ways. We see this on a national scale; the United States has reaped the blessings that our forefathers procured by faith and prayer. Many are not living for God today, yet are blessed with freedom and safety because of God's promise to show mercy to thousands. We see the opposite of this in foreign lands where the people worship heathen gods and idols and where the curses of poverty, sickness, filth and ignorance are rampant. Even so in our personal lives we inherit the blessing or the curse, dependent upon our parents' relationship with God.

Timothy in the New Testament received the blessing of faith from his mother and grandmother because they were devoted Christians. **(2 Timothy 1:5, When I call to remembrance the unfeigned faith that is in thee, which dwelt first in thy grandmother Lois, and thy mother Eunice: and I am persuaded that in thee also.).**

Our New Father

We do not have a problem understanding how we inherit physical and emotional traits from our parents and grandparents, but some people cannot believe we inherit spiritual traits although the Word teaches otherwise. In the natural, if a father should have weak kidneys, many times the children will have this same problem. If the parents are highly nervous and fearful, the children will, many times, have these same characteristics. Should a parent have an addictive personality, the children can inherit that trait also. Spiritually we encounter the same kind of situation. As a child of God, we do not have to keep those things that are detrimental to our lives, because we have a new Father. We now can receive the Heavenly Father's traits, His healings and His blessings.

We no longer inherit the curse. We must, however, appropriate the blessings. They are not automatic. We should ask the Lord in prayer to break every "chain of iniquity" over our lives and disinherit the evil things from our earthly parents so as to receive the blessings promised to those that love God.

The Choice Is Ours

The curses and the blessings are recorded in **Deuteronomy 27, 28, and 30**. We are told to choose which one we receive.

I call heaven and earth to record this day against you,

that I have set before you life and death, blessing and cursing: therefore choose life, that both thou and thy seed may live: That thou mayest love the Lord thy God, and that thou mayest obey his voice, and that thou mayest cleave unto him: for he is thy life, and the length of thy days: that thou mayest dwell in the land which the Lord sware unto thy fathers, to Abraham, to Isaac and to Jacob, to give them (Deuteronomy 30:19-20).

We can see in these three chapters that financial blessings, physical blessings, favor with man, spiritual blessings and others are ours if we follow the Lord and His ways. Conversely, if we do not resist the devil and break the hold he has had on us through our parents, we can be under his curse of sickness, poverty and fear. Christ died and was made a curse for us so that we might have life more abundantly.

Christ hath redeemed us from the curse of the law, being made a curse for us: for it is written, Cursed is every one that hangeth on a tree: That the blessing of Abraham might come on the Gentiles through Jesus Christ; that we might receive the promise of the Spirit through faith....And if ye be Christ's, then are ye Abraham's seed, and heirs according to the promise (Galatians 3:13-14, 29).

Curses

The "chain of iniquity" is not the only kind of curse that must be overcome. There are times when curses are spoken against people by those who practice witchcraft. As children of God we need not be afraid of these affecting us since Satan has no power to bring evil upon us unless we are practicing sin and are living out of the will of God. Those, however, who are outside of Christ and His protection, can suffer terrible effects from these evil practices. A satanic curse is designed as a stumbling block to cause Christians to fall, thus leading to their destruction. False prophets, sorcerers, witches and other emissaries of the devil cast spells and place curses on people. This was spoken of in the Bible as we are told of their diabolical ways.

Having eyes full of adultery, and that cannot cease from sin; beguiling unstable souls: an heart they have exercised with covetous practices; cursed children: which have forsaken the right way, and are gone astray, following the way of Balaam the son of Bosor, who loved the wages of unrighteousness; But was rebuked for his iniquity: the dumb ass speaking with man's voice forbad the madness of the prophet. These are wells without water, clouds that are carried with a tempest; to whom the mist of darkness is reserved for ever (2 Peter 2:14-17).

In this Scripture we see that unstable souls and those who have forsaken following the Lord are affected by a curse pronounced against them.

Balaam was the son of a soothsayer (one who practices witchcraft, **Joshua 13:22**). God hates this practice now as much as He did then. Balaam began as a prophet of God but ended up as a false prophet. One of the reasons was probably because of the chain of iniquity from his father's participation in witchcraft. Balaam yielded to sin and false doctrine. (**Numbers 22,23,24, & 31:16**).

Curses not only can affect people directly, but also indirectly and can cause people to stumble unless they watch and pray. Christians who do not know and use their authority over the devil and his curses can be adversely affected without realizing the root cause of their problems.

But I have a few things against thee, because thou hast there them that hold the doctrine of Balaam, who taught Balac to cast a stumbling block before the children of Israel, to eat things sacrificed unto idols, and to commit fornication. So hast thou also them that hold the doctrine of the Nicolaitans, which thing I hate. Repent; or else I will come unto thee quickly, and will fight against them with the sword of my

mouth. He that hath an ear, let him hear what the Spirit saith unto the churches... (Revelation 2:14-17).

Curses Turned to Blessings

If we repent of our sin and obey the Lord, we need never fear a curse coming against us. We must realize that lack of prayer is sinfulness and can allow the enemy to come against us; so we should be sure that we put on the whole armour of God. If we do this, then every curse can be turned into a blessing for us as children of God. **...because they hired against thee Balaam the son of Beor of Pethor of Mesopotamia, to curse thee. Nevertheless the Lord thy God would not hearken unto Balaam; but the Lord thy God turned the curse into a blessing unto thee, because the Lord thy God loved thee (Deuteronomy 23:4-5).**

Prayer can break this kind of curse easily if we know how to pray. Some people teach that one should send a curse back to those who pronounced it in order to be free. This is simply not according to Scripture, as the Word of God teaches we are to overcome evil with good, not evil with evil.

Bless them which persecute you: bless, and curse not...Recompense to no man evil for evil....Be not overcome of evil, but overcome evil with good (Romans 12:14, 17, and 21).

Bless them that curse you, and pray for them which despitefully use you (Luke 6:28).

We should pray a prayer similar to the following to be set free from any curse, "Father, in Jesus' name we submit ourselves to you. We use the authority that you have given us, and we command the enemy to release his hold on us. We break every curse and negative prayer that has been said against us. We ask you to be merciful and forgive these people. Lord; open their eyes to see the truth and set them free from the bondage of Satan. We destroy the plans of the enemy against our lives and declare that we have the protection of your guardian angels around us. We claim your Word in **Psalm 91** that says, **Surely he shall deliver thee from the snare of the fowler...There shall no evil befall thee...For he shall give his angels charge over thee, to keep thee in all thy ways.**

We trust in your Word, Lord, and we shall not walk in fear, but in the victory and the power of the Holy Spirit. Amen."

4

The Spiritual Warfare Battle

Two Spiritual Worlds

God has given us mighty weapons with which to fight the devil, and we need not be discouraged or fearful that we cannot overcome him. One of Satan's main devices, however, is to keep people ignorant of him and his demons.

We must understand the existence of a spiritual world. Actually this world is more real than the physical one, for the Bible declares the earth shall one day pass away; however, the spiritual world will last forever. In that world there are two kingdoms: the kingdom of light ruled by God and the kingdom of darkness ruled by Satan. Satan's eventual destiny is to be chained and cast into the bottomless pit of hell. All those that choose his evil ways will also be chained with him. Those that choose Christ will partake in His righteous kingdom of heaven forever.

We Are in a War

Although at present Satan is ruling here on earth, he is no match for a child of God who knows his authority in Christ. However, these people are in the minority, as spiritual ignorance is rampant today. Due to this unawareness, it is easy for the devil to slander God and discourage man. Most people do not fully understand we are truly in a war. They pray earnestly for the Lord to answer their prayers, yet do not understand they must follow certain principles to receive their requests.

An example of this would be for a man with a financial need to come to the bank president pleading for monetary help. The man knows nothing about banking procedures, especially concerning the third party of depositors and directors. He sees his problem as strictly between himself and the bank official. "You've got the money and I need it; why not let me have it?" the man cries. The banker's explanations and expressions of regret only add to the man's discontent. In reference to prayer, if we are not aware of the spiritual laws in operation and spiritual wickedness in high places (principalities and powers), we too may blame God if we do not get an immediate answer to our prayers.

For though we walk in the flesh, we do not war after the flesh: (For the weapons of our warfare are not carnal, but mighty through God to the pulling down of strong holds;) (II Corinthians 10:3-4).

Spiritual Warfare

Many times, there are certain things we must do before we can receive our answers. Then again, it may simply be a matter of time before our answers come as it was with Daniel. In **Daniel 10** we read there was a delay of three weeks between the time God heard Daniel's prayer and the time God spoke to him. There was a war going on in the heavens that tried to prevent Daniel's answer from coming, but because of his faith and fasting the answer did come. Battling to win takes effort and time.

Then said he (an angel) unto me, Fear not, Daniel: for from the first day that thou didst set thine heart to understand, and to chasten thyself before thy God, thy words were heard, and I am come for thy words. But the prince of the kingdom of Persia withstood me one and twenty days: but, lo, Michael, one of the chief princes, came to help me; and I remained there with the kings of Persia (Daniel 10:12-13).

The angels and fallen angels are both referred to as "princes" and "kings" in these verses. These angels had a battle in the heavens because of Daniel's prayers.

Today we have been challenged to stand up in the Lord's

army and fight the same kind of spiritual battles. Paul was a New Testament saint who fought spiritual battles and won, and he encouraged Timothy to do likewise.

I have fought a good fight, I have finished my course, I have kept the faith... (2 Timothy 4:7).

This charge I commit unto thee, son Timothy, according to the prophecies which went before on thee, that thou by them mightest war a good warfare... (I Timothy 1:18).

How do we fight in this battle, and what are our weapons? Let us look at **Ephesians 6:10-18** for our answers.

Finally, my brethren, be strong in the Lord, and in the power of his might. Put on the whole armour of God, that ye may be able to stand against the wiles of the devil. For we wrestle not against flesh and blood, but against principalities, against powers, against the rulers of the darkness of this world, against spiritual wickedness in high places. Wherefore take unto you the whole armour of God, that ye may be able to withstand in the evil day, and having done all, to stand. Stand therefore, having your loins girt about with truth, and having on the breastplate of righteousness; And your feet shod with the preparation of the gospel of peace; Above all, taking the shield of faith, wherewith ye shall be able to quench all the fiery darts of the wicked. And take the helmet of salvation, and the sword of the Spirit, which is the word of God: Praying always with all prayer and supplication in the Spirit, and watching thereunto with all perseverance and supplication for all saints...

This epistle was written to the Christians at Ephesus, but is also for us as Christians today. We must realize we are in a spiritual battle as long as we are on this earth.

This Scripture starts out by admonishing us to **...be strong in the Lord and in the power of his might**. We do not have to depend on our strength, for it is no match for the devil. It is the name of Jesus and His power that gives us victory over the devil. We must put on the whole armour to be sure of our victory because the devil is waiting to discover any cracks in it. He is full of wiles and tricks.

The Battleground Is the Mind

The battleground is in the mind. Satan brings lewd thoughts and temptations to our minds and we must know how to deal with them. Looking again at **2 Corinthians 10:3-5**, we find our battle is against wicked imaginings that Satan sends.

For though we walk in the flesh, we do not war after the flesh: (For the weapons of our warfare are not carnal, but mighty through God to the pulling down of strongholds;) Casting down imaginations, and every high thing that exalteth itself against the knowledge of God, and bringing into captivity every thought to the obedience of Christ.

This war in which we are engaged is not in the flesh, but in the spirit. When we have a thought that is alien to God's Word, we must learn to deal with it as from the enemy if we are to get the victory. When we have thoughts of resentment, jealousy, pride, hatred, bitterness, fear, doubt, unbelief, depression, sorrow, lust or greed, we must recognize that these do not come from our precious Lord, but originate from the pit of hell.

Thoughts Become Actions

God wants us to be filled with His love, peace, health, joy and faith, so we know anything opposite to these cannot be His suggestions. Therefore, the first step to getting the victory over the enemy is to recognize him. We must immediately rebuke evil thoughts and command the devil to leave with his wicked suggestions. We must not allow them to stay in our minds, but rather "cast them down." It is not sinful to have a fleeting evil thought as that is the way Satan comes to tempt us; however, the sin is when we allow the thought to stay and muse on it, and allow it to settle into our hearts. When we do this, eventually we put that thought into action. We are told to guard our hearts in **Proverbs 4:23, Keep thy heart with all diligence; for out of it are the issues of life.**

Satan comes against the thought life of many beautiful Christians and condemns them for even thinking the things he brings to their minds. These defiling thoughts come many times during a worship service or during times of prayer and are designed to distract them from the Lord. They must take authority over the devil and command him to leave, taking with him his evil and condemnation, and recognize him as the source of these mental pictures. Sometimes these are so vile and evil one would be embarrassed to mention them to anyone. They need not be tormented any longer if they know how to deal with the devil. Once they have discovered the enemy's wiles and understand that he works in certain patterns, they will be able to quickly get rid of him. They must not allow these evil thoughts to take root in their minds but resist them so that they will flee. If they take root, then they must be dealt with differently, as a root is more difficult to dig out than a fleeting thought.

Halloween Is an Evil Holiday

Evil suggestions are not the only ones we are to resist, but all things that do not agree with the Word of God. Since our carnal minds are full of the world's ideas and traditions, we must learn to resist these also in order to allow the Holy Spirit to implant His truth in our hearts. We must seek the true doctrine of God's Word and let men's traditions go. **But in vain they do worship me, teaching for doctrines the commandments of men (Matthew 15:9).**

One very evil tradition is the celebration of Halloween. No Christian should partake in the activities of this holiday, nor should they allow their children to do so. We can discern the evil of this day by taking a look at the festivities that are associated with its celebration. Children are dressed as witches, goblins, ghosts, little devils and fortune tellers. All these are representatives of Satan's kingdom. Games played at carnivals promote fear in children as they are ushered through spook houses and horror rooms. Skeletons, black cats and bats represent death and darkness. No carnival is complete without the gypsy who tells fortunes. Satan has gained man's approval to celebrate his day by simply making it a tradition that seems like a fun day. The opposite is true, however, as more damage and harm are done on this day each year than any other holiday. Children are taught to go door to door chanting "trick or treat." It is unchristian to demand a gift under threat of playing some trick. Police are on the alert for juvenile vandalism and caution parents to be watchful.

Satanists celebrate this as their high holy day and even offer human sacrifices to the devil. Until recently, most Christians have not questioned this traditional celebration, but rather have gone along with it by even bringing Halloween parties into the church. The earliest Halloween celebrations were held by, not the early church, but the Druids in honor of Samhain, the Lord of the Dead, and his demons, whose festival fell on November 1. Halloween actually means "holy or hallowed evening." (According to the Roman calendar in which days began at midnight, the evening of October 31 was the eve before the hallowed day, hence Halloween or All Soul's Eve was kept throughout the ancient pagan world.).

It can also be called All Hallows Eve because it is the day before All Hallows' or All Saints' day, a holy day in the Roman Catholic Church, Episcopal Church, the Church of England and the Greek Orthodox Church. This festival honors all martyrs, known and unknown, who have died for the church. During the time of Constantine, these two holidays were merged in an attempt to Christianize the heathen. The church could not prevent these heathen practices, so they thought "taming" them would be the answer. They were, of course, not to worship their gods on the church's All Saint's day. However, as it is with all compromises, soon the evil overrode the good, and hence we still honor these heathen practices by celebrating Halloween.

Evil in Some Traditions

Satan has also infiltrated and defiled our Christian celebration of Christmas by adding the dimension of Santa Claus to the celebration of the Saviour's birth. Due to this and other error, some argue we should not even observe Christmas since December 25 is not the true birth date of our Lord Jesus Christ, as most scholars agree it was in the fall. However, the date is not important but the attitude of our hearts in celebrating it. Since it is observed around the world, it is a wonderful time to witness to people, and the holiday does cause some to think of Jesus.

Satan perverts that date because he hates to see people worshipping the Lord. That is why he has interjected "Old Saint Nicholas" or "Santa Claus" to take away from the true meaning of Christmas. Santa Claus is portrayed as a god. He supposedly "knows all" as does God. ("He knows when you are sleeping, he knows when you're awake, he knows when you've been bad or good...") He has supernatural power as he flies through the air making stops throughout the world in one night. He comes down chimneys that would be impossible to enter and has an unlimited supply of toys in one sleigh. The belief in Santa Claus is based on a lie. This lie by parents undermines the trust of their children. Later the children may then doubt the reality of God because parents lied about Santa Claus. The emphasis is on receiving gifts in many homes, instead of exchanging gifts. Gifts for the Lord are forgotten.

As Christians, we need to purge this holiday of Satan's false god, Santa Claus, and put the emphasis on Christ and His love. Some may say how terrible to deny children the fun of Santa Claus, and many cannot believe that he is inspired by Satan. However, if we ask why Santa Claus is promoted at Christmas instead of another day of the year, I believe we can see the answer clearly. We should celebrate Christmas every day of the year, instead of once a year as the world does. It does not take tinsel and decoration to remind us of Jesus when we truly love and worship Him from our hearts.

Easter is another Christian holiday that Satan has managed to tarnish with his introduction of bunnies and Easter eggs. This is another tradition we never think to question. We simply go along with it, teaching our children the fun of gathering eggs instead of the true meaning of Easter, Christ's resurrection from the dead.

The origin of eggs and bunnies stems back to pagan "fertility" rites. The Persians, Egyptians, and Germans instigated these old traditions. Our eyes have been taken off the real meaning of these holidays, and we are caught up in the things of the world instead of worshiping the Lord. Actually the holiday of Easter is named after a Semitic goddess of fertility and sexual love named Astarte.

We need to keep Christ not only in the center of our holidays, but also in the center of every day of the year. We should celebrate Christ's resurrection each day by allowing that same resurrected life to flow through us. Man should not judge us as to how we celebrate holidays or even sabbath days as we are admonished to recognize these as only shadows of the real life in Christ.

Let no man therefore judge you in meat, or in drink, or in respect of an holyday, or of the new moon, or of the sabbath days: Which are a shadow of things to come; but the body is of Christ (Colossians 2:16-17).

Actively Resist the Devil

To stand against the wiles of the devil, we must actively resist him and he will flee. The Bible does not say ignore the devil

and he will flee, but rather resist him. The passivity and complacency of many Christians have allowed the devil to ravage their
lives. The only thing necessary for evil to prevail is for the good
to do nothing. We should be totally involved with the things of
God instead of fostering complacency.

Ephesians 6:12 says, **For we wrestle not against flesh and
blood, but against principalities, against powers, against the
rulers of the darkness of this world, against spiritual wickedness in high places.** Notice, this verse states we are in a "wrestling match." This shows us that there is a struggle involved to
overcome the enemy. We must understand our battle is not with
people, but rather with the evil spirits working through them.

Since all truth runs in parallels, and we know that the Holy
Spirit operates through people, Satan works through people also.
This does not mean they are of the devil, but that they are under
the devil's influence. We all have, at times, yielded to the devil and
been his instruments. We do not want to continue to do this once
we know the Lord; that is why we resist Satan.

We find an example of this happening to one of Jesus' disciples. This is recorded in **Mark 8:30-33, And he charged them
that they should tell no man of him. And he began to teach
them, that the Son of man must suffer many things, and be
rejected of the elders, and of the chief priests, and scribes,
and be killed, and after three days rise again. And he spake
that saying openly. And Peter took him, and began to rebuke
him. But when he had turned about and looked on his disciples, he rebuked Peter, saying, Get thee behind me, Satan:
for thou savourest not the things that be of God, but the things
that be of men.**

Don't Speak Satan's Words

Jesus was speaking to Peter here when He rebuked the devil,
for He recognized that Peter was speaking under Satan's influ-

ence. This did not mean Peter was of the devil, but rather a devil was speaking through him, as we see later in his life he became an overcomer, and people who were merely in his shadow were healed.

Insomuch that they brought forth the sick into the streets, and laid them on beds and couches, that at the least the shadow of Peter passing by might overshadow some of them (Acts 5:15).

Jesus also recognized the influence of the Holy Spirit on Peter as well as Satan's influence because just prior to this Peter had proclaimed the Lord Jesus as the Christ.

And Simon Peter answered and said, Thou art the Christ, the Son of the living God. And Jesus answered and said unto him, Blessed art thou, Simon Barjona: for flesh and blood hath not revealed it unto thee, but my Father which is in heaven (Matthew 16:16-17).

The verse below is a beautiful example of how Jesus handled the problem of the enemy coming through His beloved disciple; after rebuking the devil and exposing this as a demonic response from Peter, He did something else. We find this in **Luke 22:31-32, And the Lord said, Simon, Simon, behold, Satan hath desired to have you, that he may sift you as wheat: But I have prayed for thee, that thy faith fail not: and when thou art converted, strengthen thy brethren.**

Jesus prayed that Peter would be set free from the devil. We can learn through this example. When our loved ones allow the enemy to work through them, we need to go to the prayer closet, rebuke the devil, and pray that they be set free from his influence.

Don't Fight People

We must realize our battle is not with people (flesh and blood), but with Satan (principalities, powers, and rulers of the darkness, (**Ephesians 6:12**). Arguing only brings strife; we must do our battling in the Spirit through prayer. Only spiritual warfare will produce peace and harmony when a spirit of division is trying to get hold of someone.

Marriages are falling apart today because people are fighting their battles in the flesh instead of using spiritual weapons to deliver their mates from Satan's hold. To obtain the victory, we must do as Jesus did and lay down our lives for our loved ones by going to prayer on their behalf when they are being led about by the devil. We must stand for them lest their faith fail and Satan "sift them as wheat." We must recognize their hurtful words as coming from Satan. Instead, so many allow Satan to use them. They retaliate and soon bite and devour one another. **For all the law is fulfilled in one word, even in this; Thou shalt love thy neighbour as thyself. But if ye bite and devour one another, take heed that ye be not consumed one of another (Galatians 5:14-15).**

Put on the Whole Armor of God

Ephesians 6:13 admonishes us, **Wherefore take unto you the whole armour of God, that ye may be able to withstand in the evil day, and having done all, to stand.** We can take one look around us and realize we are in the "evil day." If we are to stand against the devil and get the victory, we must take on the whole life of God.

Not every Christian will still be standing after Satan's onslaughts, for the Bible says some shall fall away. **They on the rock are they, which, when they hear, receive the word with joy; and these have no root, which for a while believe, and in time of temptation fall away (Luke 8:13).**

As Christians, we come into warfare regardless of whether we desire to fight or not. That is why it is imperative to equip ourselves for the battle. When we are "babes" in Christ, the Lord takes care of our needs and puts His shield over us. He does not require us to enter into great spiritual battles for which we have no preparation. However, we are not to remain "babes," but we are to grow in Him and in His strength and take our place among the saints of God, who have learned to overcome the devil and his onslaughts.

Dress for Battle

Let us look at the armour we are to put on in **Ephesians 6:14-18, Stand therefore, having your loins girt about with truth...1 Peter 1:13** gives us a definition of the "loins." **Wherefore gird up the loins of your mind, be sober, and hope to the end for the grace that is to be brought unto you at the revelation of Jesus Christ.** We are to gird the loins of our mind with truth. Jesus and His Word are truth, so this Scripture means that we are to allow Jesus to rule our minds and we are to read God's Word. As we read and study God's Word and fellowship with Him, we soon will find our thinking changed.

Our task is to put the Word into our minds; God's part is to transfer it from our minds to our hearts. If we are truly fellowshipping with the Lord, we will not allow a day to go by without reading the Bible. In fact, this is a good gauge that can reveal our relationship with God. If we love the Lord, we will love His Word.

Satan Resists God's Word

Satan tries to hinder us from reading God's Word as he knows, better than most, the power and strength that is gained by giving the Word of God priority. We need to be on guard and recognize Satan's lies in this area. He will tell us, "You cannot understand what you are reading, so why read the Bible?" or, "This is not ministering to you, and you cannot even keep your mind on it, so why read it?" These are only a few of his lies to try to keep us out of the Word. If we are faithful and continue to read regardless of our mental understanding, we will push past that difficulty because it will minister to our spirits regardless of our comprehension. We must take the Word in us, so that the Holy Spirit will have something to "quicken" to us when we need a Word from the Lord.

Another lie Satan tells some is that the early Christians did not have Bibles and God spoke to them, so we don't need Bibles today. The disciples taught the first-century Christians God's Word as they had studied under Jesus. When a Christian has no access to God's Word, the Lord can supernaturally teach them His Word. This is rare, however, as God's Word has circled the globe. Nevertheless some underground Christians have testified of this miracle.

Food for the Spirit Is the Word

God's Word is spiritual food to our spirit man, just as natural food is sustenance to our physical bodies. If we do not feed our spirits, soon they become weak and lifeless. Jesus is the "Bread of Life" and we must partake of Him to have His life flowing in us.

And Jesus said unto them, I am the bread of life: he that cometh to me shall never hunger; and he that believeth on me shall never thirst (John 6:35).

If we are filled with God's Word we shall be satisfied. Many are filling their minds with "garbage" they have taken in through television, secular magazines and harmful movies. It is no wonder many Christians are sick, weak and on the verge of moral collapse. If they would spend as many hours studying and reading God's Word as they do watching TV, we would see the church making a greater impact on this world.

We Must Control the Emotions

Not only are we to have our minds girded with truth, but also "having on the breastplate of righteousness" is a requirement. A breastplate covers the heart area. Symbolically this would mean our emotions should be covered with Christ's righteousness. One of Satan's main targets is to strike us in our emotions, and if we do not know our standing in Christ, he will succeed at condemning us and discouraging us.

First of all, we must define the word righteousness according to the Greek definition. It means to be "just" or "right" before God, or to be in "right standing" with Him. The Bible declares in **Romans 3:10, ...There is none righteous, no, not one** and in **Isaiah 64:6, But we are all as an unclean thing, and all our righteousnesses are as filthy rags....** If we are all unrighteous, then how do we put on the breastplate of righteousness?

We receive this righteousness at the moment we receive Christ. Through His death and resurrection we can now have eternal life and His righteousness.

To wit, that God was in Christ, reconciling the world unto himself, not imputing their trespasses unto them; and hath committed unto us the word of reconciliation. Now then we are ambassadors for Christ, as though God did beseech you by us: we pray you in Christ's stead, be ye reconciled to God. For he hath made him to be sin for us, who knew no sin; that we might be made the righteousness of God in him (2 Corinthians 5:19-21).

Repenting of our sin and asking Jesus to come into our hearts puts us in "right standing" with God. We must realize we are now righteous if we are a born-again Christian and must no longer allow Satan to condemn us. **There is therefore now no condemnation to them which are in Christ Jesus, who walk not after the flesh, but after the Spirit (Romans 8:1).**

Of course, we grow in God's righteousness as we continue

to walk in Him; thus we become holy. However, by faith we are righteous the moment we receive Jesus. We have access to the throne of God and can approach our Father because the blood of Jesus has cleansed us from all unrighteousness. When Satan comes with the lies of "You can't expect God to answer your prayer because you sinned yesterday," and "He will not answer but will punish you," we will recognize it for what it is--a lie. We know when we ask God to forgive us that He does not hold anything against us and He forgets our sins. **And their sins and iniquities will I remember no more (Hebrews 10:17).** If God does not remember our sins anymore, then we should not allow Satan to remind us of them after we have asked for forgiveness. This is putting on the breastplate of righteousness. We declare by faith we are righteous because of what Jesus has done and command the devil to depart along with his accusations.

The Gospel of Peace

Next, in **Ephesians 6**, we come to **verse 15, And your feet shod with the preparation of the gospel of peace**. This part of our armour keeps our walk with God as it should be. We are to spread the gospel of peace. We are to be peacemakers. This has a two-fold application. First, we are to share Jesus with others, bringing them to the "Prince of Peace." Through Him sinners find peace with God. **Therefore being justified by faith, we have peace with God through our Lord Jesus Christ (Romans 5:1).**

Second, we are to be peacemakers among men. **Endeavouring to keep the unity of the Spirit in the bond of peace (Ephesians 4:3). Blessed are the peacemakers: for they shall be called the children of God (Matthew 5:9).** We are not to sow seeds of discord among the brethren which causes enmity, but we are to be peace-makers. If we have a problem with a brother or sister in Christ, we are to strive to resolve it and keep peace and unity in the body of Christ.

95

Faith Is Our Shield

The next piece of armour listed is a most important one also. It is the "shield of faith." **Above all, taking the shield of faith, wherewith ye shall be able to quench all the fiery darts of the wicked (Eph. 6:16).** Satan is continually sending his flaming missiles of temptations, accusations, sicknesses, depressions, fears, doubts, etc. To overcome these, we must have our faith centered in Christ and His Word.

If we do anything not of faith, it is sin, so we must make every move as an act of faith in the Lord. **...for whatsoever is not of faith is sin (Romans 14:23).** Godly faith is trusting and believing God simply because He says something is true, in spite of what our situation looks like. When the devil tempts us to doubt God's integrity and His Word, we use our shield of faith to put out that fiery dart. Faith is so important it is listed not only here as part of our armour but also it is a fruit of the spirit as well as a gift of the spirit.

Mind Guarded by the Word

The next piece of our warring attire is our helmet of salvation. **And take the helmet of salvation (Ephesians 6:17).** The helmet protects our thought life. Satan bombards our minds with evil from all directions. We need to guard our minds by being careful what we hear and see. **(Mark 4:24, ...take heed what ye hear...).**

Rock and worldly music can cause extreme nervousness and rebellion. We must not allow this to enter our spirits. If we are exposed to this unintentionally, we need to ask the Father to filter out the effects as we put on our helmet of salvation. We must be careful what we see through television and other media. Many television programs are satanic and we can receive demonic influences through them. *Bewitched* is one that goes undetected as satanic because it seems to be such a cute little show. However, it prepares children and adults to receive witchcraft in its other forms. Anything that has to do with the devil, darkness, and dark mysterious powers, we should turn off. We must use our spiritual helmet to save us from the enemy's attacks against our minds. We must guard our children's minds also as even seemingly cute cartoons and funny books are full of witchcraft and evil influences.

The Word Is Our Sword

We can now use our offensive weapon, the sword. **...And the sword of the Spirit, which is the word of God (Ephesians 6:17).** Up until now, we have used only defensive weapons. Numerous Christians never take any territory for God, but exist only by hiding under their "shield of faith," and using the sword only to beat off the enemy when he attacks. This is not the highest purpose of God. We are to live victorious Christian lives. Instead, many Christians confess what a terrible time they have with the devil and how the devil is always after them. It should be the other way around.

We should be constantly after the devil. He should tremble when he sees a Christian because the power that Jesus had is the same power that dwells in us through the Holy Spirit.

But if the Spirit of him that raised up Jesus from the dead dwell in you, he that raised up Christ from the dead shall also quicken your mortal bodies by his Spirit that dwelleth in you (Romans 8:11).

If that power was able to raise Christ from the dead, is it not able to cause demons to flee, heal sick bodies, and overcome any obstacle in the path of a Christian? He is able if we use the weapons He has given us. We are to take His Word and let it become such a part of us that nothing can hinder us in our walk with the Lord.

Nay, in all these things we are more than conquerors through him that loved us" (Romans 8:37). John 15:7 declares, **If ye abide in me, and my words abide in you, ye shall ask what ye will, and it shall be done unto you.**

The sword of the Spirit, which is His Word, causes the enemy not only to flee, but also to give up territory he has had in our lives and in the lives of others. Jesus, when he was tempted, overcame the devil by quoting the Word to him. Satan tried to get Him to turn the stones into bread since Jesus had been fasting forty days and nights. **But he answered and said, It is written, Man shall not live by bread alone, but by every word that proceedeth out of the mouth of God (Matthew 4:4).** From this statement by Jesus, we can see how important God's Word is to us if we are to get the victory.

Prayer Overcomes

After putting on this armour we are then given our "marching orders." **Ephesians 6:18** says, **Praying always with all prayer and supplication in the Spirit, and watching thereunto with all perseverance and supplication for all saints.** Prayer is a necessary key to overcoming the devil. This verse says to pray with all prayer and supplication "in the Spirit." This is referring to "praying in tongues" or "praying in the Spirit."

For he that speaketh in an unknown tongue speaketh not unto men, but unto God: for no man understandeth him; howbeit in the spirit he speaketh mysteries (1 Corinthians 14:2).

We are to use both kinds of prayer to overcome Satan: the prayer "in the Spirit" (tongues) and the prayer of understanding. Paul was an overcomer and he said, **I thank my God, I speak with tongues more than ye all (1 Corinthians 14:18).**

Many times as we pray we become quite loud as we rebuke the devil and command him to leave. War is not quiet. We must be strong and aggressive against the devil because he does not like to give up territory he has had. We should use wisdom, however, when we battle in the Spirit since unbelievers and those that are not acquainted with speaking in tongues might be offended.

If therefore the whole church be come together into one place, and all speak with tongues, and there come in those that are unlearned, or unbelievers, will they not say that ye are mad? (1 Corinthians 14:23).

One of Satan's current devices is to discount the power of praying in tongues. He tells people this gift is not for today. The nine spiritual gifts in **1 Corinthians 12** are just as valid today as they were then, and just as needed. How can we believe these are not for us, when we need healing today, wisdom today, and knowledge today? We also need the gift of speaking in tongues today.

God does not want us to walk in spiritual ignorance concerning the gifts. **Now concerning spiritual gifts, brethren, I would not have you ignorant (1 Corinthians 12:1)**. We must search the Word of God to see what the Scripture says about the gifts, not just believe what man has to say about them. If we keep a proper heart attitude before God and desire to know the truth about the gifts of the Spirit, the Lord will reveal it to us.

Should you be one who is seeking the truth, I would urge you not to seek out man's opinions because if you ask fifteen different people about the gifts of the Holy Spirit (especially the gift of speaking in tongues), you will receive fifteen different opinions.

If we seek the Heavenly Father and search His Word with an open heart and mind, He not only will reveal to us the truth, but also will lead us into all truth. It is only when we hold on to our traditional ideas and maintain an air of spiritual pride, that we become unteachable. Let us come before the Father as little children, trusting Him to give us only good and beautiful gifts. **Luke 11:13** says, **If ye then, being evil, know how to give good gifts unto your children: how much more shall your heavenly Father give the Holy Spirit to them that ask him?**

We are told to persevere in our prayers. We are not to give up, but are to maintain our position in Christ and hold fast to His Word. We do not have to continue to battle after we have "prayed through" on a certain thing, but we must continue to stand and believe until that prayer is answered. The Lord may also reveal other ways in which we are to pray for certain situations.

We are not only to be persistent in prayer, but also disciplined in our prayer life. **Ephesians 6:18** says, **Praying always...** We must ask God to help us have good prayer habits. A careless prayer life can leave room for the devil to get the victory. Notice too, we are admonished to have "supplication for all saints." We must not just be concerned for "me" and "mine," but reach out to all the family of God with our prayers. As we stand for one another in unity, we will see the enemy flee from all of us. We must continue in steadfastness until we get the victory we are promised. If we have put on all this armor, yet still have not overcome, we need to ask the Lord for the key that will bring our victory.

Jesus Is the Head

In this hour, when gross darkness has covered the earth, we need God's protection and His guidance. **Romans 13:12** says, **The night is far spent, the day is at hand: let us therefore cast off the works of darkness, and let us put on the armor of light.** The armor is the light of Jesus Christ and this is what we are to put on. We are to put away the works of darkness. When we have the light of Jesus Christ, we have the light of God, the whole armor. Light gives us knowledge to see the works of darkness and enables us to see the path Jesus would have us walk. We can defeat the devil and rise above the things of this earth to walk in heavenly places.

May this Scripture be a prayer for you: **That the God of our Lord Jesus Christ, the Father of glory, may give unto you the spirit of wisdom and revelation in the knowledge of him: The** eyes of your understanding being enlightened; that ye may know what is the hope of his calling, and what the riches of the glory of his inheritance in the saints, And what is the exceeding greatness of his power to us-ward who believe, according to the working of his mighty power, Which he wrought in Christ, when he raised him from the dead, and set him at his own right hand in the heavenly places, Far above all principality, and power, and might, and dominion, and every name that is named, not only in this world, but also in that which is to come: And hath put all things under his feet, and gave him to be the head over all things to the church, Which is his body, the fullness of him that filleth all in all (Ephesians 1:17-23).

Church, let us go forth victoriously!

Index

Additional Books by the Author:

Book Titles in the OVERCOMING LIFE SERIES:

PROVE ALL THINGS
THE TRUE GOD
THE WILL OF GOD
KEYS TO THE KINGDOM
EXPOSING SATAN'S DEVICES
HEALING OF THE SPIRIT, SOUL & BODY
NEITHER MALE NOR FEMALE
EXTREMES OR BALANCE?
THE PATHWAY INTO THE OVERCOMER'S WALK

Book Titles in the END TIMES SERIES:

MARK OF GOD OR MARK OF THE BEAST
PERSONAL SPIRITUAL WARFARE

For on-line orders, please visit our website:

http://www.BibleResources.org

Christ Unlimited Ministries, Inc.
P.O. Box 850
Dewey, AZ 86327
U.S.A.

Postnote

The Millers are very glad to receive mail from their readers; however, they are unable to answer the letters personally due the volume of mail that they receive. They will be happy to pray along with their intercessors for all who write with a prayer request; although they do no outside counseling as they believe this should be directed to local pastors as outlined in Scripture.

Christ Unlimited Ministries, Inc. is a non-profit church 501(c) (3) corporation. All contributions are tax deductible. We appreciate your prayers, encouragement and support. Your purchase of this book makes it possible for us to share free copies of Bibles, teaching literature, tracts and downloadable audio/video materials with ministers in third world countries who would otherwise not be able to purchase them.

The Lord gave the word: great was the company of those that published it (Psalm 68:11).

For Additional Study

This book is taken from a course of Bible studies called the Overcoming Life Series. The entire series is a virtual "spiritual tool chest," as it covers a multitude of subjects every Christian faces in his walk with God. It also answers questions that many believers have concerning the current move of God. These are dealt with in a balanced approach and in the light of the Scripture. God's people are not to live frustrated, defeated lives, but rather they are to be victorious overcomers! Other books available with their companion workbooks are:

PROVE ALL THINGS - Christ warned that great deception would be one of the signs of the end times. In this book, instruction is given on how to recognize false prophets and teachings. Clear Scriptural guidelines are given on discerning the Spirit of truth versus the spirit of error. The book deals with how to judge without being judgmental.

THE TRUE GOD - This is a teaching on the character of God, explaining why God does certain things, and why it is against His nature to do other things. It differentiates between the things for which God is responsible and the things for which the devil is responsible. Our responsibility as Christians destined to overcome is made clear so that we can live victorious lives.

THE WILL OF GOD - This lesson teaches us not only how to know the will of God in our personal lives, family, ministry and finances, but also brings understanding as to why God allows sin, sickness and suffering in the world. As overcomers, Christians are not to suffer under many of the things we have accepted as normal.

KEYS TO THE KINGDOM - Instruction on how to gain authority in God's Kingdom through prayer is the topic of this book. Many principles and methods of prayer are covered, such as praying in the Spirit, fasting and prayer, travailing prayer, praise, intercession and spiritual warfare.

EXPOSING SATAN'S DEVICES - This book is a powerful expose' of Satan's tricks, tactics and lies. Cult and Occultic methods and groups are listed so Christians can detect their activity. Demon activity is discussed and deliverance and casting out demons is dealt with in detail. Satan's kingdom is uncovered and the Christian is taught to overcome through spiritual discernment and warfare.

HEALING OF THE SPIRIT, SOUL AND BODY - This book teaches how to overcome emotional problems, as well as physical ones, and how to receive divine healing. It also teaches how to renew the carnal mind and walk in the spirit of life, thereby overcoming depression, loneliness and fear.

NEITHER MALE NOR FEMALE - What is the woman's role in the church and home? Who is a woman's spiritual head and covering? Does God call women to the five-fold ministry? What does God's Word say about divorce, celibacy and choosing a marriage partner? These and other woman related topics are Scripturally examined.

EXTREMES OR BALANCE? - Many Christians have hurt the cause of Christ through "out-of-balance" teachings and demonstrations. This book shows how to avoid those areas. It also deals wisely with the excesses and extremes in the body of Christ.

THE PATHWAY INTO THE OVERCOMER'S WALK - This book contains answers to the questions an overcomer faces as he presses toward the prize of the high calling in Christ Jesus. How can we be conformed to the image of Christ? How does the Holy Spirit work with the overcomers in the end times? What are the overcomer's rewards?

PERSONAL SPIRITUAL WARFARE - Explains the invisible world of spiritual forces that influence our lives and how good can prevail over the evil around us as we prepare for the new kingdom age that is coming. This book will help you overcome problems in your finances, marriage, the emotional pressures of fear, anger and hurt. Here are the keys to victory through spiritual warfare.

MARK OF GOD OR MARK OF THE BEAST - Much has been written and said about the mark of the beast, but little has been said about the mark of God. What does the 666 mean and what is this mysterious mark? How is it linked to the world of finance? Has this mark already begun? This book answers many questions about the mark of the beast and the mark of God, and how they affect Christians.

Please visit our web site for information on how to order the complete "Overcoming Life Bible Study." Our site is also and excellent source for additional books and Bible resources.

www.BibleResources.org

Purpose and Vision

Go ye therefore, and teach all nations, baptiz-
ing them in the name of the Father, and of the Son,
and of the Holy Ghost: Teaching them to observe
all things whatsoever I have commanded you: and,
lo, I am with you alway, even unto the end of the
world. Amen.

Matthew 28:19,20

Christ Unlimited is not "another denomination," sect, or just
a separate group. It is an arm of the Body of Christ — the Church
of Jesus Christ, which has been called to strengthen the Body at
large. We also believe we have been called to help establish the
Kingdom of God in the earth.

Christ Unlimited is involved with all Bible-believing Christians regardless of their church or denominational affiliations and
committed to helping wherever possible in evangelistic and teaching outreaches.

Christ Unlimited believes that time is running out and the
Gospel has not been preached to every creature. Many nations
have not heard the Gospel, and in many places, doors for evange-
lism are closing. We believe it is time all Christians cooperated
with the Lord in breaking down denominational walls for a united
front line against the kingdom of darkness and in setting up the
Kingdom of the Lord Jesus Christ by the power of the Holy Spirit.

Christ Unlimited provides such tools as to enable the saints
of God to establish the Kingdom of God in the earth. We encourage groups of prayer warriors who will pray, fast, and intercede
for the nations. This, we believe, is weapon number one. We teach
believers how to overcome through spiritual warfare and through

111

knowing how to use their authority in Christ Jesus through the Word and the power of the Holy Spirit.

Christians need to know how to bring down the forces of darkness in their own lives and in the lives of those to whom they minister. We provide such tools as Bibles, literature, Christ Unlimited books and an online prayer ministry. We publish the Gospel going forth via any means of communication, including the Internet, videos, as well as literature. We have teaching seminars, Bible schools, and correspondence courses, all aimed at winning souls to Christ and building the Body of Christ into maturity.

Bud and Betty Miller serve the Lord together as founders of the multi-visioned ministry outreach, Christ Unlimited. The outreaches of this ministry have stemmed from a tremendous desire to see the Word of God taught in its balanced entirety. The Millers are firm believers in prayer and, through prayer, have seen many released from the bondages of fear, failure, and defeat.

The outreaches of Christ Unlimited are in obedience to the words of our Lord in **Mark 16:15**: **Go ye into all the world and preach the gospel to every creature.** This mandate from the Lord presents a challenge to our generation as an estimated 25 percent of the world's population still have not heard the Good News of Jesus Christ.

Christ Unlimited Ministries also is dedicated to teaching God's Word. **Hosea 4:6** says: **My people are destroyed for lack of knowledge.** Many Christians are leading defeated lives simply because they do not know God's Word in its fullest.

Christ Unlimited Ministries has provided for those who desire to know God's Word in a greater way. The main thrust of the teaching and literature is directed at "How to be an overcomer." In the endtimes, we must be prepared to overcome the onslaughts of Satan. Many Christians are suffering needlessly, because they do not know how to overcome sickness, depression, divorce, fear, and financial failure. Christ Unlimited Ministries provides answers for troubled families as well as trains workers for service.

www.ingramcontent.com/pod-product-compliance
Lightning Source LLC
Chambersburg PA
CBHW020949030426
42339CB00004B/23